Anonymous

Messages of the President on the relations of the United States to Spain

and also transmitting consular correspondencce respecting the condition of the reconcentrados in Cuba

Anonymous

Messages of the President on the relations of the United States to Spain
and also transmitting consular correspondencce respecting the condition of the reconcentrados in Cuba

ISBN/EAN: 9783744731461

Printed in Europe, USA, Canada, Australia, Japan

Cover: Foto ©ninafisch / pixelio.de

More available books at **www.hansebooks.com**

MESSAGE

OF THE

PRESIDENT OF THE UNITED STATES,

COMMUNICATED TO THE

TWO HOUSES OF CONGRESS,

ON THE

RELATIONS OF THE UNITED STATES TO SPAIN

BY REASON OF

WARFARE IN THE ISLAND OF CUBA.

APRIL 11, 1898.—Read, referred to the Committee on Foreign Affairs, and ordered to be printed.

WASHINGTON:
GOVERNMENT PRINTING OFFICE.
1898.

MESSAGE.

To the Congress of the United States:

Obedient to that precept of the Constitution which commands the President to give from time to time to the Congress information of the state of the Union and to recommend to their consideration such measures as he shall judge necessary and expedient, it becomes my duty now to address your body with regard to the grave crisis that has arisen in the relations of the United States to Spain by reason of the warfare that for more than three years has raged in the neighboring island of Cuba.

I do so because of the intimate connection of the Cuban question with the state of our own Union and the grave relation the course which it is now incumbent upon the nation to adopt must needs bear to the traditional policy of our Government if it is to accord with the precepts laid down by the founders of the Republic and religiously observed by succeeding Administrations to the present day.

The present revolution is but the successor of other similar insurrections which have occurred in Cuba against the dominion of Spain, extending over a period of nearly half a century, each of which, during its progress, has subjected the United States to great effort and expense in enforcing its neutrality laws, caused enormous losses to American trade and commerce, caused irritation, annoyance, and disturbance among our citizens, and, by the exercise of cruel, barbarous, and uncivilized practices of warfare, shocked the sensibilities and offended the humane sympathies of our people.

Since the present revolution began, in February, 1895, this country has seen the fertile domain at our threshold ravaged by fire and sword in the course of a struggle unequaled in the history of the island and rarely paralleled as to the numbers of the combatants and the bitterness of the contest by any revolution of modern times where a dependent people striving to be free have been opposed by the power of the sovereign state.

Our people have beheld a once prosperous community reduced to comparative want, its lucrative commerce virtually paralyzed, its exceptional productiveness diminished, its fields laid waste, its mills in ruins, and its people perishing by tens of thousands from hunger and destitution. We have found ourselves constrained, in the observance of that strict neutrality which our laws enjoin, and which the law of nations commands, to police our own waters and watch our own seaports in prevention of any unlawful act in aid of the Cubans.

Our trade has suffered; the capital invested by our citizens in Cuba has been largely lost, and the temper and forbearance of our people have been so sorely tried as to beget a perilous unrest among our own citizens which has inevitably found its expression from time to time in the National Legislature, so that issues wholly external to our own body politic engross attention and stand in the way of that close devotion to domestic advancement that becomes a self-contained commonwealth whose primal maxim has been the avoidance of all foreign entanglements. All this must needs awaken, and has, indeed, aroused the utmost concern on the part of this Government, as well during my predecessor's term as in my own.

In April, 1896, the evils from which our country suffered through the Cuban war became so onerous that my predecessor made an effort to bring about a peace through the mediation of this Government in any way that might tend to an honorable adjustment of the contest between Spain and her revolted colony, on the basis of some effective scheme of self-government for Cuba under the flag and sovereignty of Spain. It failed through the refusal of the Spanish Government then in power to consider any form of mediation or, indeed, any plan of settlement which did not begin with the actual submission of the insurgents to the mother country, and then only on such terms as Spain herself might see fit to grant. The war continued unabated. The resistance of the insurgents was in no wise diminished.

The efforts of Spain were increased, both by the dispatch of fresh levies to Cuba and by the addition to the horrors of the strife of a new and inhuman phase happily unprecedented in the modern history of civilized Christian peoples. The policy of devastation and concentration, inaugurated by the Captain-General's bando of October 21, 1896, in the Province of Pinar del Rio was thence extended to embrace all of the island to which the power of the Spanish arms was able to reach by occupation or by military operations. The peasantry, including all dwelling in the open agricultural interior, were driven into the garrison towns or isolated places held by the troops.

The raising and movement of provisions of all kinds were interdicted. The fields were laid waste, dwellings unroofed and fired, mills destroyed, and, in short, everything that could desolate the land and render it unfit for human habitation or support was commanded by one or the other of the contending parties and executed by all the powers at their disposal.

By the time the present administration took office a year ago, reconcentration—so called—had been made effective over the better part of the four central and western provinces, Santa Clara, Matanzas, Havana, and Pinar del Rio

The agricultural population to the estimated number of 300,000 or more was herded within the towns and their immediate vicinage, deprived of the means of support, rendered destitute of shelter, left poorly clad, and exposed to the most unsanitary conditions. As the scarcity of food increased with the devastation of the depopulated areas of production, destitution and want became misery and starvation. Month by month the death rate increased in an alarming ratio. By March, 1897, according to conservative estimates from official Spanish sources, the mortality among the recoucentrados, from starvation and the diseases thereto incident, exceeded 50 per centum of their total number.

No practical relief was accorded to the destitute. The overburdened towns, already suffering from the general dearth, could give no aid. So-called "zones of cultivation" established within the immediate areas of effective military control about the cities and fortified camps proved illusory as a remedy for the suffering. The unfortunates, being for the most part women and children, with aged and helpless men, enfeebled by disease and hunger, could not have tilled the soil without tools, seed, or shelter for their own support or for the supply of the cities. Reconcentration, adopted avowedly as a war measure in order to cut off the resources of the insurgents, worked its predestined result. As I said in my message of last December, it was not civilized warfare; it was extermination. The only peace it could beget was that of the wilderness and the grave.

Meanwhile the military situation in the island had undergone a noticeable change. The extraordinary activity that characterized the second year of the war, when the insurgents invaded even the thitherto unharmed fields of Pinar del Rio and carried havoc and destruction up to the walls of the city of Havana itself, had relapsed into a dogged struggle in the central and eastern provinces. The Spanish arms regained a measure of control in Pinar del Rio and parts of Havana, but, under the existing conditions of the rural country, without immediate improvement of their productive situation. Even thus partially restricted, the revolutionists held their own, and their conquest and submission, put forward by Spain as the essential and sole basis of peace, seemed as far distant as at the outset.

In this state of affairs my Administration found itself confronted with the grave problem of its duty. My message of last December reviewed the situation and narrated the steps taken with a view to relieving its acuteness and opening the way to some form of honorable settlement. The assassination of the prime minister, Canovas, led to a change of government in Spain. The former administration, pledged to subjugation without concession, gave place to that of a more liberal party, committed long in advance to a policy of reform involving the wider principle of home rule for Cuba and Puerto Rico.

The overtures of this Government, made through its new envoy,

General Woodford, and looking to an immediate and effective amelioration of the condition of the island, although not accepted to the extent of admitted mediation in any shape, were met by assurances that home rule, in an advanced phase, would be forthwith offered to Cuba, without waiting for the war to end, and that more humane methods should thenceforth prevail in the conduct of hostilities. Coincidentally with these declarations, the new Government of Spain continued and completed the policy already begun by its predecessor, of testifying friendly regard for this nation by releasing American citizens held under one charge or another connected with the insurrection, so that, by the end of November, not a single person entitled in any way to our national protection, remained in a Spanish prison.

While these negotiations were in progress the increasing destitution of the unfortunate reconcentrados and the alarming mortality among them claimed earnest attention. The success which had attended the limited measure of relief extended to the suffering American citizens among them by the judicious expenditure through the consular agencies of the money appropriated expressly for their succor by the joint resolution approved May 24, 1897, prompted the humane extension of a similar scheme of aid to the great body of sufferers. A suggestion to this end was acquiesced in by the Spanish authorities. On the 24th of December last, I caused to be issued an appeal to the American people, inviting contributions in money or in kind for the succor of the starving sufferers in Cuba, following this on the 8th of January by a similar public announcement of the formation of a central Cuban relief committee, with headquarters in New York City, composed of three members representing the American National Red Cross and the religious and business elements of the community.

The efforts of that committee have been untiring and have accomplished much. Arrangements for free transportation to Cuba have greatly aided the charitable work. The president of the American Red Cross and representatives of other contributory organizations have generously visited Cuba and cooperated with the consul-general and the local authorities to make effective distribution of the relief collected through the efforts of the central committee. Nearly $200,000 in money and supplies has already reached the sufferers and more is forthcoming. The supplies are admitted duty free, and transportation to the interior has been arranged, so that the relief, at first necessarily confined to Havana and the larger cities, is now extended through most, if not all of the towns where suffering exists.

Thousands of lives have already been saved. The necessity for a change in the condition of the reconcentrados is recognized by the Spanish Government. Within a few days past the orders of General Weyler have been revoked; the reconcentrados, it is said, are to be permitted to return to their homes, and aided to resume the self-supporting pursuits of peace. Public works have been ordered to give them employment, and a sum of $600,000 has been appropriated for their relief.

The war in Cuba is of such a nature that short of subjugation or extermination a final military victory for either side seems impracticable. The alternative lies in the physical exhaustion of the one or the other party, or perhaps of both—a condition which in effect ended the ten years' war by the truce of Zanjon. The prospect of such a protraction and conclusion of the present strife is a contingency hardly to be contemplated with equanimity by the civilized world, and least of all by the United States, affected and injured as we are, deeply and intimately, by its very existence.

Realizing this, it appeared to be my duty, in a spirit of true friendliness, no less to Spain than to the Cubans who have so much to lose by the prolongation of the struggle, to seek to bring about an immediate termination of the war. To this end I submitted, on the 27th ultimo, as a result of much representation and correspondence, through the United States minister at Madrid, propositions to the Spanish Government looking to an armistice until October 1 for the negotiation of peace with the good offices of the President.

In addition, I asked the immediate revocation of the order of reconcentration, so as to permit the people to return to their farms and the needy to be relieved with provisions and supplies from the United States, cooperating with the Spanish authorities, so as to afford full relief.

The reply of the Spanish cabinet was received on the night of the 31st ultimo. It offered, as the means to bring about peace in Cuba, to confide the preparation thereof to the Insular Parliament, inasmuch as the concurrence of that body would be necessary to reach a final result, it being, however, understood that the powers reserved by the constitution to the Central Government are not lessened or diminished. As the Cuban Parliament does not meet until the 4th of May next, the Spanish Government would not object, for its part, to accept at once a suspension of hostilities if asked for by the insurgents from the general in chief, to whom it would pertain, in such case, to determine the duration and conditions of the armistice.

The propositions submitted by General Woodford and the reply of the Spanish Government were both in the form of brief memoranda, the texts of which are before me, and are substantially in the language above given. The function of the Cuban Parliament in the matter of "preparing" peace and the manner of its doing so are not expressed in the Spanish memorandum; but from General Woodford's explanatory reports of preliminary discussions preceding the final conference it is understood that the Spanish Government stands ready to give the Insular Congress full powers to settle the terms of peace with the insurgents—whether by direct negotiation or indirectly by means of legislation does not appear.

With this last overture in the direction of immediate peace, and its disappointing reception by Spain, the Executive is brought to the end of his effort.

In my annual message of December last I said:

> Of the untried measures there remain only: Recognition of the insurgents as belligerents; recognition of the independence of Cuba; neutral intervention to end the war by imposing a rational compromise between the contestants, and intervention in favor of one or the other party. I speak not of forcible annexation, for that can not be thought of. That, by our code of morality, would be criminal aggression.

Thereupon I reviewed these alternatives, in the light of President Grant's measured words, uttered in 1875, when after seven years of sanguinary, destructive, and cruel hostilities in Cuba he reached the conclusion that the recognition of the independence of Cuba was impracticable and indefensible; and that the recognition of belligerence was not warranted by the facts according to the tests of public law. I commented especially upon the latter aspect of the question, pointing out the inconveniences and positive dangers of a recognition of belligerence which, while adding to the already onerous burdens of neutrality within our own jurisdiction, could not in any way extend our influence or effective offices in the territory of hostilities.

Nothing has since occurred to change my view in this regard; and I recognize as fully now as then that the issuance of a proclamation of neutrality, by which process the so-called recognition of belligerents is published, could, of itself and unattended by other action, accomplish nothing toward the one end for which we labor—the instant pacification of Cuba and the cessation of the misery that afflicts the island.

Turning to the question of recognizing at this time the independence of the present insurgent government in Cuba, we find safe precedents in our history from an early day. They are well summed up in President Jackson's message to Congress, December 21, 1836, on the subject of the recognition of the independence of Texas. He said:

> In all the contests that have arisen out of the revolutions of France, out of the disputes relating to the Crowns of Portugal and Spain, out of the separation of the American possessions of both from the European Governments, and out of the numerous and constantly occurring struggles for dominion in Spanish America, so wisely consistent with our just principles has been the action of our Government, that we have, under the most critical circumstances, avoided all censure, and encountered no other evil than that produced by a transient estrangement of good will in those against whom we have been by force of evidence compelled to decide.
>
> It has thus made known to the world that the uniform policy and practice of the United States is to avoid all interference in disputes which merely relate to the internal government of other nations, and eventually to recognize the authority of the prevailing party without reference to our particular interests and views or to the merits of the original controversy.
>
> * * * But on this, as on every other trying occasion, safety is to be found in a rigid adherence to principle.
>
> In the contest between Spain and the revolted colonies we stood aloof, and waited not only until the ability of the new States to protect themselves was fully established, but until the danger of their being again subjugated had entirely passed away. Then, and not until then, were they recognized.

Such was our course in regard to Mexico herself. * * * It is true that with regard to Texas the civil authority of Mexico has been expelled, its invading army defeated, the chief of the Republic himself captured, and all present power to control the newly organized government of Texas annihilated within its confines; but, on the other hand, there is, in appearance at least, an immense disparity of physical force on the side of Texas. The Mexican Republic, under another Executive, is rallying its forces under a new leader and menacing a fresh invasion to recover its lost dominion.

Upon the issue of this threatened invasion the independence of Texas may be considered as suspended; and were there nothing peculiar in the relative situation of the United States and Texas, our acknowledgment of its independence at such a crisis could scarcely be regarded as consistent with that prudent reserve with which we have hitherto held ourselves bound to treat all similar questions.

Thereupon Andrew Jackson proceeded to consider the risk that there might be imputed to the United States motives of selfish interest in view of the former claim on our part to the territory of Texas, and of the avowed purpose of the Texans in seeking recognition of independence as an incident to the incorporation of Texas in the Union, concluding thus:

Prudence, therefore, seems to dictate that we should still stand aloof and maintain our present attitude, if not until Mexico itself, or one of the great foreign powers shall recognize the independence of the new government, at least until the lapse of time or the course of events shall have proved beyond cavil or dispute the ability of the people of that country to maintain their separate sovereignty and to uphold the government constituted by them. Neither of the contending parties can justly complain of this course. By pursuing it we are but carrying out the long-established policy of our Government, a policy which has secured to us respect and influence abroad and inspired confidence at home.

These are the words of the resolute and patriotic Jackson. They are evidence that the United States, in addition to the test imposed by public law as the condition of the recognition of independence by a neutral state (to wit, that the revolted state shall "constitute in fact a body politic, having a government in substance as well as in name, possessed of the elements of stability," and forming de facto, "if left to itself, a state among the nations, reasonably capable of discharging the duties of a state"), has imposed for its own governance in dealing with cases like these the further condition that recognition of independent statehood is not due to a revolted dependency until the danger of its being again subjugated by the parent state has entirely passed away.

This extreme test was, in fact, applied in the case of Texas. The Congress to whom President Jackson referred the question as one "probably leading to war," and therefore a proper subject for "a previous understanding with that body by whom war can alone be declared and by whom all the provisions for sustaining its perils must be furnished," left the matter of the recognition of Texas to the discretion of the Executive, providing merely for the sending of a diplomatic agent when the President should be satisfied that the Republic of Texas had become "an independent State." It was so recognized by President Van Buren, who commissioned a chargé d'affaires March 7, 1837, after

Mexico had abandoned an attempt to reconquer the Texan territory, and when there was at the time no bona fide contest going on between the insurgent Province and its former Sovereign.

I said in my message of December last, "It is to be seriously considered whether the Cuban insurrection possesses beyond dispute the attributes of statehood which alone can demand the recognition of belligerency in its favor." The same requirement must certainly be no less seriously considered when the graver issue of recognizing independence is in question, for no less positive test can be applied to the greater act than to the lesser; while, on the other hand, the influences and consequences of the struggle upon the internal policy of the recognizing State, which form important factors when the recognition of belligerency is concerned, are secondary, if not rightly eliminable, factors when the real question is whether the community claiming recognition is or is not independent beyond peradventure.

Nor from the standpoint of expediency do I think it would be wise or prudent for this Government to recognize at the present time the independence of the so-called Cuban Republic. Such recognition is not necessary in order to enable the United States to intervene and pacify the island. To commit this country now to the recognition of any particular government in Cuba might subject us to embarrassing conditions of international obligation toward the organization so recognized. In case of intervention our conduct would be subject to the approval or disapproval of such government. We would be required to submit to its direction and to assume to it the mere relation of a friendly ally.

When it shall appear hereafter that there is within the island a government capable of performing the duties and discharging the functions of a separate nation, and having, as a matter of fact, the proper forms and attributes of nationality, such government can be promptly and readily recognized and the relations and interests of the United States with such nation adjusted.

There remain the alternative forms of intervention to end the war, either as an impartial neutral by imposing a rational compromise between the contestants, or as the active ally of the one party or the other.

As to the first, it is not to be forgotten that during the last few months the relation of the United States has virtually been one of friendly intervention in many ways, each not of itself conclusive, but all tending to the exertion of a potential influence toward an ultimate pacific result, just and honorable to all interests concerned. The spirit of all our acts hitherto has been an earnest, unselfish desire for peace and prosperity in Cuba, untarnished by differences between us and Spain, and unstained by the blood of American citizens.

The forcible intervention of the United States as a neutral to stop the war, according to the large dictates of humanity and following many historical precedents where neighboring States have interfered to check the hopeless sacrifices of life by internecine conflicts beyond their borders, is justifiable on rational grounds. It involves, however, hostile constraint upon both the parties to the contest as well to enforce a truce as to guide the eventual settlement.

The grounds for such intervention may be briefly summarized as follows:

First. In the cause of humanity and to put an end to the barbarities, bloodshed, starvation, and horrible miseries now existing there, and which the parties to the conflict are either unable or unwilling to stop or mitigate. It is no answer to say this is all in another country, belonging to another nation, and is therefore none of our business. It is specially our duty, for it is right at our door.

Second. We owe it to our citizens in Cuba to afford them that protection and indemnity for life and property which no government there can or will afford, and to that end to terminate the conditions that deprive them of legal protection.

Third. The right to intervene may be justified by the very serious injury to the commerce, trade, and business of our people, and by the wanton destruction of property and devastation of the island.

Fourth, and which is of the utmost importance. The present condition of affairs in Cuba is a constant menace to our peace, and entails upon this Government an enormous expense. With such a conflict waged for years in an island so near us and with which our people have such trade and business relations—when the lives and liberty of our citizens are in constant danger and their property destroyed and themselves ruined—where our trading vessels are liable to seizure and are seized at our very door by war ships of a foreign nation, the expeditions of filibustering that we are powerless to prevent altogether, and the irritating questions and entanglements thus arising—all these and others that I need not mention, with the resulting strained relations, are a constant menace to our peace, and compel us to keep on a semiwar footing with a nation with which we are at peace.

These elements of danger and disorder already pointed out have been strikingly illustrated by a tragic event which has deeply and justly moved the American people. I have already transmitted to Congress the report of the naval court of inquiry on the destruction of the battle ship *Maine* in the harbor of Havana during the night of the 15th of February. The destruction of that noble vessel has filled the national heart with inexpressible horror. Two hundred and fifty-eight brave sailors and marines and two officers of our Navy, reposing in the fancied security of a friendly harbor, have been hurled to death, grief and want brought to their homes and sorrow to the nation.

The naval court of inquiry, which, it is needless to say, commands the unqualified confidence of the Government, was unanimous in its conclusion that the destruction of the *Maine* was caused by an exterior explosion, that of a submarine mine. It did not assume to place the responsibility. That remains to be fixed.

In any event the destruction of the *Maine*, by whatever exterior cause, is a patent and impressive proof of a state of things in Cuba that is intolerable. That condition is thus shown to be such that the Spanish Government can not assure safety and security to a vessel of the American Navy in the harbor of Havana on a mission of peace, and rightfully there.

Further referring in this connection to recent diplomatic correspondence, a dispatch from our minister to Spain, of the 26th ultimo, contained the statement that the Spanish minister for foreign affairs assured him positively that Spain will do all that the highest honor and justice require in the matter of the *Maine*. The reply above referred to of the 31st ultimo also contained an expression of the readiness of Spain to submit to an arbitration all the differences which can arise in this matter, which is subsequently explained by the note of the Spanish minister at Washington of the 10th instant, as follows:

> As to the question of fact which springs from the diversity of views between the reports of the American and Spanish boards, Spain proposes that the facts be ascertained by an impartial investigation by experts, whose decision Spain accepts in advance.

To this I have made no reply.

President Grant, in 1875, after discussing the phases of the contest as it then appeared, and its hopeless and apparent indefinite prolongation, said:

> In such event, I am of opinion that other nations will be compelled to assume the responsibility which devolves upon them, and to seriously consider the only remaining measures possible—mediation and intervention. Owing, perhaps, to the large expanse of water separating the island from the peninsula, * * * the contending parties appear to have within themselves no depository of common confidence, to suggest wisdom when passion and excitement have their sway, and to assume the part of peacemaker.
>
> In this view in the earlier days of the contest the good offices of the United States as a mediator were tendered in good faith, without any selfish purpose, in the interest of humanity and in sincere friendship for both parties, but were at the time declined by Spain, with the declaration, nevertheless, that at a future time they would be indispensable. No intimation has been received that in the opinion of Spain that time has been reached. And yet the strife continues with all its dread horrors and all its injuries to the interests of the United States and of other nations.
>
> Each party seems quite capable of working great injury and damage to the other, as well as to all the relations and interests dependent on the existence of peace in the island; but they seem incapable of reaching any adjustment, and both have thus far failed of achieving any success whereby one party shall possess and control the island to the exclusion of the other. Under these circumstances, the agency of others, either by mediation or by intervention, seems to be the only alternative which must sooner or later be invoked for the termination of the strife.

In the last annual message of my immediate predecessor during the pending struggle, it was said:

> When the inability of Spain to deal successfully with the insurrection has become manifest, and it is demonstrated that her sovereignty is extinct in Cuba for all pur-

poses of its rightful existence, and when a hopeless struggle for its reestablishment has degenerated into a strife which means nothing more than the useless sacrifice of human life and the utter destruction of the very subject-matter of the conflict, a situation will be presented in which our obligations to the sovereignty of Spain will be superseded by higher obligations, which we can hardly hesitate to recognize and discharge.

In my annual message to Congress, December last, speaking to this question, I said:

The near future will demonstrate whether the indispensable condition of a righteous peace, just alike to the Cubans and to Spain, as well as equitable to all our interests so intimately involved in the welfare of Cuba, is likely to be attained. If not, the exigency of further and other action by the United States will remain to be taken. When that time comes that action will be determined in the line of indisputable right and duty. It will be faced, without misgiving or hesitancy, in the light of the obligation this Government owes to itself, to the people who have confided to it the protection of their interests and honor, and to humanity.

Sure of the right, keeping free from all offense ourselves, actuated only by upright and patriotic considerations, moved neither by passion nor selfishness, the Government will continue its watchful care over the rights and property of American citizens and will abate none of its efforts to bring about by peaceful agencies a peace which shall be honorable and enduring. If it shall hereafter appear to be a duty imposed by our obligations to ourselves, to civilization and humanity to intervene with force, it shall be without fault on our part and only because the necessity for such action will be so clear as to command the support and approval of the civilized world.

The long trial has proved that the object for which Spain has waged the war can not be attained. The fire of insurrection may flame or may smolder with varying seasons, but it has not been and it is plain that it can not be extinguished by present methods. The only hope of relief and repose from a condition which can no longer be endured is the enforced pacification of Cuba. In the name of humanity, in the name of civilization, in behalf of endangered American interests which give us the right and the duty to speak and to act, the war in Cuba must stop.

In view of these facts and of these considerations, I ask the Congress to authorize and empower the President to take measures to secure a full and final termination of hostilities between the Government of Spain and the people of Cuba, and to secure in the island the establishment of a stable government, capable of maintaining order and observing its international obligations, insuring peace and tranquillity and the security of its citizens as well as our own, and to use the military and naval forces of the United States as may be necessary for these purposes.

And in the interest of humanity and to aid in preserving the lives of the starving people of the island I recommend that the distribution of food and supplies be continued, and that an appropriation be made out of the public Treasury to supplement the charity of our citizens.

The issue is now with the Congress. It is a solemn responsibility. I have exhausted every effort to relieve the intolerable condition of affairs which is at our doors. Prepared to execute every obligation imposed upon me by the Constitution and the law, I await your action.

Yesterday, and since the preparation of the foregoing message, official information was received by me that the latest decree of the Queen Regent of Spain directs General Blanco, in order to prepare and facilitate peace, to proclaim a suspension of hostilities, the duration and details of which have not yet been communicated to me.

This fact with every other pertinent consideration will, I am sure, have your just and careful attention in the solemn deliberations upon which you are about to enter. If this measure attains a successful result, then our aspirations as a Christian, peace-loving people will be realized. If it fails, it will be only another justification for our contemplated action.

WILLIAM McKINLEY.

EXECUTIVE MANSION, *April 11, 1898.*

CONSULAR CORRESPONDENCE RESPECTING THE CONDITION
OF THE RECONCENTRADOS IN CUBA, THE STATE OF
THE WAR IN THAT ISLAND, AND THE PROS-
PECTS OF THE PROJECTED AUTONOMY.

MESSAGE

FROM THE

PRESIDENT OF THE UNITED STATES,

TRANSMITTING

IN RESPONSE TO THE RESOLUTION OF THE SENATE, DATED FEBRUARY 14,
1898, CALLING FOR INFORMATION IN RESPECT TO THE CONDITION OF
THE RECONCENTRADOS IN CUBA, THE STATE OF THE WAR
AND THE COUNTRY, AND THE PROSPECTS OF PRO-
JECTED AUTONOMY IN THAT ISLAND.

APRIL 11, 1898.—Read, referred to the Committee on Foreign
Relations, and ordered to be printed.

WASHINGTON:
GOVERNMENT PRINTING OFFICE.
1898.

To the Senate of the United States:

I transmit herewith, in response to a resolution of the Senate of the 14th of February last calling for information and correspondence in regard to the condition of the Island of Cuba and to negotiations for commercial relations between the United States and that island, a report of the Secretary of State, with its accompanying correspondence covering the first inquiry of the resolution, together with a report of the special commissioner plenipotentiary charged with commercial negotiations under the provisions of the tariff act approved July 24, 1897, in response to the second inquiry.

WILLIAM MCKINLEY.

EXECUTIVE MANSION,
Washington, April 11, 1898.

The PRESIDENT:

The Secretary of State has had the honor to receive, by reference from the President, a resolution adopted in the Senate of the United States on the 14th of February last, reading as follows:

Resolved, That the President is requested, if in his opinion it is not incompatible with the public service, to send to the Senate copies of the reports of the consul-general and of the consuls of the United States in Cuba, written or received since March fourth, eighteen hundred and ninety-seven, which relate to the state of war in that island and the condition of the people there, or that he will send such parts of said reports as will inform the Senate as to these facts.

Second. That the President inform the Senate whether any agent of a government in Cuba has been accredited to this Government or the President of the United States with authority to negotiate a treaty of reciprocity with the United States, or any other diplomatic or commercial agreement with the United States, and whether such person has been recognized and received as the representative of such government in Cuba.

This resolution contemplates answer being made to two separate inquiries: First, in relation to the present condition of affairs in Cuba, and, secondly, with regard to the action had in view of the overtures of the Government of Spain for a reciprocal commercial agreement covering, particularly, the trade between the United States and the Island of Cuba.

The conduct of commercial negotiations under the authority and in accordance with the conditions found in sections 3, 4, and 5 of the existing tariff act approved July 24, 1897, having been intrusted to a special commissioner plenipotentiary duly empowered by the President to that end, it has been deemed convenient to leave to the commissioner the preparation of a report in answer to the second part of the Senate resolution, the undersigned reserving to himself the response to the first part thereof, which concerns the political and consular functions of the Department of State. The separate report of the Hon. John A. Kasson, special commissioner plenipotentiary, is therefore herewith independently submitted to the President with a view to its transmission to the Senate, should such a course be, in the Presidents' judgment, not incompatible with the public service.

The Senate resolution, while in terms calling for the submission to that honorable body of all or of a practical selection of the reports of the consul-general and consuls of the United States in Cuba written or received since March 4, 1897, which relate to the state of war in that island and the condition of the people there, appears to leave it to the discretion of the President to direct the scope of the information to be so reported and the manner of its communication. The undersigned, having taken the President's direction on both these points, has the honor to lay before him a selection of the correspondence received by the Department of State from the various consular representatives in Cuba, aiming thereby to show the present situation in the island rather than to give a historical account of all the reported incidents since the date assigned by the resolution.

Respectfully submitted.

JOHN SHERMAN.

DEPARTMENT OF STATE,
Washington, April 11, 1898.

DEPARTMENT OF STATE, WASHINGTON,
Office of Special Commissioner Plenipotentiary.

The PRESIDENT:

In response to the following resolution of the Senate, passed under date of February 14, 1898, and which was referred to the undersigned for report, viz:

Second. That the President inform the Senate whether any agent of a government in Cuba has been accredited to this Government or the President of the United States, with authority to negotiate a treaty of reciprocity with the United States, or any other diplomatic or commercial agreement with the United States; and whether such person has been recognized and received as the representative of such government in Cuba.

I have the honor to submit the following report:

In October, 1897, the minister of Spain at this capital verbally advised the undersigned that, so soon as the new Government in Spain had leisure to take up the question, he would probably be authorized to enter into negotiations with the undersigned for reciprocal trade arrangements with Spain, and that a representative of Cuba would probably be associated for the interests of that island.

Under date of December 9, 1897, the minister of the United States at Madrid was instructed to ascertain the disposition of the Spanish Government in respect to these negotiations.

Under date of January 24, 1898, a dispatch from Mr. Woodford (referred to this office) advised the Secretary of State that arrangements were made for the negotiation of a commercial treaty between Spain and the United States; that separate provisions would be made for Cuba; and that the Cuban insular government would appoint a delegate to represent that island in the negotiations. This was accompanied by a memorandum from the Spanish minister of colonies, stating that the same rules as for Cuba might be applied to Puerto Rico, and suggesting a basis for the negotiations. This communication was referred to this office on the 4th of February.

On the 6th of February, the Spanish minister, Mr. Dupuy de Lome, called on the undersigned, and announced that he was authorized to represent Spain in the pending negotiations, and that a special representative would arrive from Cuba, under appointment of the insular government, to act as far as the interests of that island were involved. He mentioned the name of Señor Angulo as the gentleman who had been suggested in Cuba for that appointment; but the delegate was not officially notified to this office.

On March 17 a note from the Spanish minister, Señor Polo de Barnabe, addressed under date of the 16th instant to the Secretary of State, was referred to this office. In that note his excellency advised this Government of his appointment by Her Majesty the Queen Regent of Spain to conduct these negotiations, assisted by Señor Manuel Rafael Angulo as special delegate of the insular government of Cuba, who would be aided by two technical assistants also appointed by the Cuban government; and, further, that an officer from the Treasury Department would be added in the same character.

His excellency announced his readiness to commence the labors of the commission so soon as the Government of the United States should formulate the general plan for carrying on the work.

Respectfully submitted, March 17, 1898.

JOHN A. KASSON,
Special Commissioner Plenipotentiary.

CORRESPONDENCE.

LIST OF DISPATCHES.

FROM HAVANA.

No. 704.—November 17, 1897, 2 inclosures.
No. 709.—November 23, 1897, 1 inclosure.
No. 710.—November 23, 1897.
No. 712.—November 27, 1897, 1 inclosure.
No. 717.—December 3, 1897.
No. 718.—December 3, 1897.
No. 723.—December 7, 1897.
No. 726.—December 13, 1897.
No. 727.—December 14, 1897.
No. 732.—December 28, 1897.
No. 733.—December 28, 1897.
Telegram—January 5, 1898.
No. 738.—January 5, 1898.
No. 742.—January 8, 1898.
No. 744.—January 13, 1898, 1 inclosure.
No. 746.—January 13, 1898, 1 inclosure.
No. 747.—January 15, 1898.
No. 749.—January 18, 1898.
No. 751.—January 21, 1898, 1 inclosure.
No. 756.—January 22, 1898.
No. 767.—February 4, 1898.
No. 773.—February 10, 1898.
Telegram—February 10, 1898.
No. 775.—February 15, 1898, 1 inclosure.
No. 785.—March 1, 1898.
Telegram—March 3, 1898.
No. 795.—March 14, 1898, 1 inclosure.
No. 797.—March 17, 1898.
Telegram—March 24, 1898.
No. 803.—March 28, 1898.
No. 809.—April 1, 1898.
No. 137.—January 10, 1898, from Cienfuegos.

FROM MATANZAS.

No. 95.—November 17, 1897.
No. 97.—December 17, 1897.
No. 99.—January 18, 1898, 1 inclosure.
No. 100.—February 8, 1898.

FROM SANTIAGO DE CUBA.

No. 405.—November 15, 1897, 1 inclosure.
No. 407.—November 20, 1897, 1 inclosure.
No. 409.—November 26, 1897.
No. 410.—December 5, 1897.

No. 413.—December 14, 1897.
No. 415.—December 21, 1897.
No. 418.—January 1, 1898.
No. 420.—January 8, 1898.
No. 421.—January 12, 1898, 1 inclosure.
No. 424.—January 22, 1898.
No. 427.—January 31, 1898.
No. 428.—February 1, 1898.
No. 432.—February 15, 1898.
No. 434.—February 16, 1898.
No. 437.—February 26, 1898, 1 inclosure.
No. 439.—March 24, 1898.

FROM SAGUA LA GRANDE.

No. 261.—November 11, 1897.
No. 264.—November 20, 1897.
No. 266.—November 25, 1897; 2 inclosures.
No. 270.—December 13, 1897; 2 inclosures.
No. 271.—December 15, 1897.
    December 28, 1897.
No. 273.—January 8, 1898; 2 inclosures.
No. 278.—January 15, 1898.
    January 10, 1898.
No. 284.—January 27, 1898.
No. 286.—January 31, 1898.
No. 288.—February 17, 1898.
No. 294.—March 12, 1898.
No. 295.—March 14, 1898.
Tel.—March 24, 1898.
No. 299.—March 24, 1898.
No. 297.—March 21, 1898.
Decrees of November 26 and 27, 1897, relating to autonomy in the Island of Cuba.

CORRESPONDENCE.

Mr. Lee to Mr. Day.

No. 704.] UNITED STATES CONSULATE-GENERAL,
Havana, November 17, 1897.

SIR: I have the honor to transmit herewith several copies, with a translation, of a decree of the Governor-General respecting the "reconcentrados," and the conditions under which they may return to their homes; and also a copy and translation of an article from La Lucha of the 15th instant, reporting an interview with me.

I am, etc.,

FITZHUGH LEE,
Consul-General.

[Inclosure No. 1, with dispatch No. 704.]

GENERAL GOVERNMENT OF THE ISLAND OF CUBA.

PROCLAMATION.

Don Ramon y Erenas, Marquis of Pena Plata, governor-general, captain-general, and general in chief of the army of this island.

Decided to afford the protection due by the Government to the country people concentrated in the towns, I have procured, by all means within the reach of the authority, to better the condition to which the rural population of this island has been reduced, more than by the direct effort of the war measures previously adopted, as a natural consequence of a violent and unjust insurrection, which, having imposed itself on this country, made itself felt from the first moment as an attempt against the national sovereignty and as a work of devastation of the country, but especially as the result of extreme passions let loose against the majority of the Cuban population, honest, active, and loyal, contended with the progress of its increasing culture, satisfied with the prosperity attained by its arts, its agriculture, industry, and commerce, proud of its race and nationality, and which after having undergone without disturbance the transformation from the work of slaves to that of freemen, offered to the world, as a special case of history, one of the most beautiful triumphs of liberty, united with the cause of order, was resolved to preserve in the noble purpose of obtaining through the evolution of ideas and by the peaceful struggles of law the consecration of its aspirations within the Spanish sovereignty.

To that purpose I have directed all the efforts which I have deemed opportune and pertinent, from ordering in a decided and conclusive manner that the reconcentrados be furnished with a daily ration and that the sick in the hospitals be duly attended, to ordering by a recent decree (bando) the reorganization of agricultural and industrial labors, as well as its normalization, to the end that without obstacles nor difficulties the poor people, specially, should be able to find means of subsistence, mitigation for their economic situation, and a possible remedy for their misfortunes.

The work of absolutely suspending the concentration and of remedying immediately the evils derived therefrom not being possible, unless it should be pretended that a crowd, composed largely of women and children, be launched into the fields, exposed, therefore, to suffer even greater evils than that which they may experience by remaining in the towns and which would surely give rise to as serious censures as the concentration measures have caused, it becomes necessary to proceed in this matter with the foresight, good sense, and tact imposed by events and which the authority can not ignore.

In view of these considerations and having resolved to make the causes of this evil disappear as far as possible, prudently, and for the benefit of all, until obtaining the complete reestablishment of the normality in the life of the rural population I have decided to order as follows:

First. All reconcentrados possessing farms, as owners, lessees, or in partnership, and who possess elements and resources to help themselves, can again establish themselves in same and commence to work, for which they shall count with the protection and aid assured to them by the last instructions regarding the reorganization of agricultural and industrial labors. To this end, they shall obtain from the proper civil or military authority the piece of land where they are to establish themselves, a permit bearing the name of the individuals composing the family, the names of the persons accompanying them, number and kind of animals which they may keep, agricultural and other implements which they may need, and the kind of labor they will undertake; and they shall at the same time prove how they will obtain the implements, clothes, and effects which they may need from the moment of their establishment.

Second. Those not comprised in such case, but who attend to the industrial and agricultural labors, as artisans and laborers, can do so, provided they reside in the farm or plantation where they work, that they pass the night within the fortified place of said farm or plantation, and that they always carry with them their proper personal documents.

Third. To this end the sugar estates, cane fields (colonias de cana), tobacco plantations, coffee plantations, and other farms or plantations of importance properly defended shall be considered as centers of labor, and their owners are authorized to have in them the necessary employees and laborers—the present reconcentrados as well as persons who having invoked pardon have complied with the formalities of surrender. Special care should be adopted that the proper hygienic measures are carried out which may guarantee the health of the laboring population.

Fourth. In all cases to which the preceding paragraphs refer to, are the owners, essees, or partners of the farms or plantations obliged to build centers of defense of the zones of cultivation which they comprehend, and in the exterior circuit of which shall be established, in compliance with orders from the general staff of the army, the basis of operations of the columns in charge of fighting the rebels and of defending such centers whenever necessary. To this end the owners, lessees, and partners of farms or plantations are authorized to carry arms for their defense, and the employees and laborers are authorized to carry revolver and machete for the defense of the zone which guarantees the elements of life to their persons and their families' subsistence—after obtaining due permission from the local authorities in accordance with the owners of the farms or plantations.

Fifth. The families and persons now concentrated who will not be able to enjoy the benefits which those comprised in the foregoing cases may obtain, either because they have no piece of land, or because they have no resources with which to establish themselves in same, or because they are unable to work, shall remain in the towns under the direct protection of the boards for the protection of the reconcentrados which shall be constituted with Government funds and with the aid of public charity.

Sixth. These boards shall be immediately organized in the capitals of the provinces by the civil governors, by the alcaldes (mayors) in the municipal districts, and by the deputies from the city governments (ayuntamientos) in the towns, and they shall act under the direction and presidency of the said civil authorities, who for the purpose of constituting said boards shall associate themselves as follows: (1) To the military commandants, who are already instructed by the general staff of their obligation to ration the reconcentrados; (2) to the parish priests, whom the ecclesiastic authority shall inform them of the cooperation they shall tender to such humane purposes; (3) to the municipal physicians, to whom pertains the medical aid of those who may need it; and (4) to the proprietors, merchants, traders, and agriculturists whom the presidents may designate.

Seventh. The protection afforded by these boards shall extend under the same conditions, not only to the reconcentrados, but to persons coming from the rebel camp and who have invoked pardon, while they lack means of subsistence.

Eighth. These boards shall report their works every fifteen days to their respective presidents or to their superiors, who in turn shall report to the secretary's office of the General Government of the island.

Ninth. The civil and military authorities in charge of the execution of these provisions shall see that they are strictly complied with, under their responsibility.

Havana, 13 November, 1897.

RAMON BLANCO.

[Inclosure No. 2, with dispatch No. 704.]

[From La Lucha, of Havana, November 15, 1897.]

MR. LEE SPEAKS.

With the arrival of the consul-general of the United States of America in this island, Mr. Fitzhugh Lee, and because of the rumors published by the press of his country regarding the attitude which the said consular representative would assume, as well as because of the report published by some Madrid paper relative to a banquet given by the New York filibusters to Mr. Lee, everything connected with the latter has again obtained a certain importance.

Yesterday, by the American steamer *Seguranca*, Mr. Lee arrived from the leave of absence granted to him by his Government.

Desirous of greeting Mr. Lee and of learning the position he would adopt in connection with the new policy which the Supreme Government intends to pursue in this island, we commissioned one of our reporters to interview the distinguished consul-general.

At dinner hour, in the hotel Inglaterra, where he stops, we approached his table and met him in company with the esteemed vice-consul, Mr. Joseph A. Springer.

After exchanging courtesies we inquired, in the first place, for his family. He told us that Mrs. and Miss Lee had remained in Virginia, one of his sons in the Military Academy of West Point, and the other one, Fitz, who accompanied him before, had a position with a railroad company.

Regarding the passage from New York to Havana he told us that he had left the former port last Wednesday, and that on Thursday the wind blew so hard that the *Seguranca*, notwithstanding her excellent conditions, rolled so much that the general fell in his stateroom, causing himself a slight wound on the forehead.

"What instructions have you received from the President?"

"I have received no special instructions of any kind," he answered. "My functions in the future shall be the same as those of the past; namely, to protect the property and lives of the American citizens in this island, and to encourage the development of the commercial interests of both countries. Nothing further."

With respect to the banquet which, according to a cablegram from New York, published by the Lucha on Saturday, had been given to him in New York by the Cuban filibusters, Mr. Lee told us that he had not attended any banquet there, and consequently made no speech; that he only remained in New York two or three days before leaving for this city, during which period he attended lunches offered to him by personal friends, with no political character whatever.

He says such a telegram is untrue, and he does not know the reason which may have inspired the author of same.

We inquired from Mr. Lee regarding the effect which the first measures of General Blanco have produced in the United States, and he told us that they had been received favorably, as would be all tending to make less sensible the horrors of the war. "In my country," he added, "peace is desired. The last words I heard from President McKinley were: 'My sincere wish is that peace be not disturbed.'"

"Aside from official circles," we inquired, "how does the American people think in regard to autonomy, about to be established in Cuba?"

"Outside of official circles," he answered, "not much is known about autonomy, and the popular classes rarely speak of it. Besides, until the new régime does not commence to act it can not be judged, and then they will see how it is received by the Cubans."

We did not wish to occupy any longer the attention of the amiable Mr. Lee, and we took leave of him, thanking him for the deferences he has always shown to the Lucha.

Mr. Lee to Mr. Day.

No. 709.] UNITED STATES CONSULATE-GENERAL,
Havana, November 23, 1897.

SIR: Someone handed me yesterday the inclosed paper, of which I accompany a translation, and which purports to be signed by the insurgent chief in command of the Havana province.

I am, etc.,

FITZHUGH LEE,
Consul-General.

[Inclosure No. 1, with Dispatch No. 709.]

WESTERN MILITARY DEPARTMENT.

To the inhabitants of Cuba:

Upon the initiation of the winter campaign by General Blanco, after the failure of the bloodthirsty Weyler, I wish to remind you of our firm resolution to continue fighting until the attainment of absolute independence.

Our principles are well defined. We wish to have a republic where all its inhabitants shall enjoy equal rights and live in fraternity. We do not hate the Spaniard. Our conduct toward the Spanish wounded and prisoners prove it. Remember "La Larga," "El Senado," "Remon de las Yaguas," "Guaimaro," and "Victoria de las Tunas" in Oriente and Camaguey, and "Lomitas" in Las Villas, as well as Vinales and "Ojo de Agua" in Pinar del Rio. Our wounded have, nevertheless, been mutilated, our prisoners shot, and the peaceful inhabitants, even women and children, murdered without pity, as if the Spanish representative, sent to Cuba by the unfortunate Canovas del Castillo, had proposed to exterminate the inhabitants of this country.

Spaniards, we only consider as enemies those who combat against us.

Cubans, do your duty and the end of the struggle will be abbreviated, and the horrors and ruins suffered by our country will terminate.

Long live the Cuban Republic!

November 10, 1897.

J. M. RODRIGUEZ,
Major-General, Chief of the Western Department.

Mr. Lee to Mr. Day.

No. 710.]
UNITED STATES CONSULATE-GENERAL,
Havana, November 23, 1897.

SIR: I have the honor to briefly submit a statement of what appears to be the present condition of affairs in this island.

First. The insurgents will not accept autonomy.

Second. A large majority of the Spanish subjects who have commercial and business interests and own property here will not accept autonomy, but prefer annexation to the United States rather than an independent republic or genuine autonomy under the Spanish flag.

Third. The Spanish authorities are sincere in doing all in their power to encourage, protect, and promote the grinding of sugar. The grinding season commences in December.

Fourth. The insurgents' leaders have given instructions to prevent grinding wherever it can be done, because by diminishing the export of sugar the Spanish Government revenues are decreased. It will be very difficult for the Spanish authorities to prevent cane burning, because one man at night can start a fire which will burn hundreds of acres, just as a single individual could ignite a prairie by throwing a match into the dry grass.

Fifth. I am confident that General Blanco, and Pando, his chief of staff, as well as Dr. Congosto, the secretary general, with all of whom I have had conversations, are perfectly conscientious in their desire to relieve the distress of those suffering from the effects of Weyler's reconcentration order, but unfortunately they have not the means to carry out such benevolent purposes.

I have read letters stating that charitable persons in the United States will send clothing, food, and some money to these unfortunate people, and I have arranged with the Ward Line of steamers to provide free transportation from New York. I hope to secure the permission of the Spanish authorities here for such things to be entered free of duty. I am told, however, that they must come consigned to the bishop of

Havana. The sufferings of the reconcentrado class have been terrible beyond description, but in Havana less than in other places on the island; yet Dr. Brunner, acting United States sanitary inspector here, informed me this morning that the death rate of the reconcentrados in this city was about 50 per cent in other places of the island, and when it is remembered that there have been several hundred thousands of these noncombatants, or pacificos, mainly women and children, who are concentrated under General Weyler's order, some idea can be formed of the mortality among them.

In this city matters are assuming better shape. Under charitable committees large numbers of them have been gathered together in houses, and are now fed and cared for by private subscriptions. I visited them yesterday and found their condition comparatively good, and there will be a daily improvement among them, though the lives of all can not be saved. I witnessed many terrible scenes and saw some die while I was present. I am told General Blanco will give $100,000 to the relief fund.

I am, etc.,
FITZHUGH LEE,
Consul-General.

Mr. Lee to Mr. Day.

No. 712.] UNITED STATES CONSULATE-GENERAL,
Havana, November 27, 1897.

SIR: One of two gentlemen who visited the reconcentrados after they were concentrated in los fosos (the ditches) in this city handed me to-day the inclosed paper. The names of these two gentlemen are not signed to it for obvious reasons.

I personally know the gentleman who brought the communication, and know that he stands high in this community as a man of integrity and character.

The number of reconcentrados here, as I had the honor to report already, have always been less than elsewhere. I am able to say now that they will be taken care of and fed by committees of charitably disposed persons.

The ayuntaminto (city government) of Havana has ordered an additional tax of 5 per cent to be levied upon real estate in this city. I am informed that this sum has already reached the amount of $80,000, and that it is to be devoted exclusively to the relief of the reconcentrados.

The $100,000 reported in a former dispatch as being given by the Governor-General, is in Spanish silver, and is to be applied to the reconcentrados over the whole island.

* * * * * * *

I am, etc.,
FITZHUGH LEE,
Consul-General.

[Inclosure with dispatch No. 712.]

SIR: The public rumor of the horrible state in which the reconcentrados of the municipal council of Havana were found in the fosos having reached us, we resolved to pay a visit there, and we will relate to you what we saw with our own eyes:

Four hundred and sixty women and children thrown on the ground, heaped pell-mell as animals, some in a dying condition, others sick and others dead, without the slightest cleanliness, nor the least help, not even to give water to the thirsty, with neither religious or social help, each one dying wherever chance laid them, and for this limited number of reconcentrados the deaths ranged between forty and fifty daily, giving relatively ten days of life for each person, with great joy to the authorities who seconded fatidically the politics of General Weyler to exterminate the Cuban people, for these unhappy creatures received food only after having been for eight days in the Fosos, if during this time they could feed themselves with the bad food that the dying refused.

On this first visit we were present at the death of an old man who died through thirst. When we arrived he begged us, for God's sake, to give him a drink. We looked for it and gave it to him, and fifteen minutes afterwards he breathed his last, not having had even a drink of water for three days before. Among the many deaths we witnessed there was one scene impossible to forget. There is still alive the only living witness, a young girl of 18 years, whom we found seemingly lifeless on the ground; on her right-hand side was the body of a young mother, cold and rigid, but with her young child still alive clinging to her dead breast; on her left-hand side was also the corpse of a dead woman holding her son in a dead embrace; a little farther on a poor, dying woman having in her arms a daughter of fourteen, crazy with pain, who after five or six days also died in spite of the care she received.

In one corner a poor woman was dying, surrounded by her children, who contemplated her in silence, without a lament or shedding a tear, they themselves being real specters of hunger, emaciated in a horrible manner. This poor woman augments the catalogue already large of the victims of the reconcentration in the fosos.

The relation of the pictures of misery and horror which we have witnessed would be never ending were we to narrate them all.

It is difficult and almost impossible to express by writing the general aspect of the inmates of the fosos, because it is entirely beyond the line of what civilized humanity is accustomed to see; therefore no language can describe it.

The circumstances which the municipal authorities could reunite there are the following: Complete accumulation of bodies dead and alive, so that it was impossible to take one step without walking over them; the greatest want of cleanliness, want of light, air, and water; the food lacking in quality and quantity what was necessary to sustain life, thus sooner putting an end to these already broken-down systems; complete absence of medical assistance; and what is more terrible than all, no consolation whatever, religious or moral.

If any young girl came in any way nice looking, she was infallibly condemned to the most abominable of traffics.

At the sight of such horrible pictures the two gentlemen who went there resolved in spite of the ferocious Weyler, who was still Captain-General of the island, to omit nothing to remedy a deed so dishonorable to humanity, and so contrary to all Christianity. They did not fail to find persons animated with like sentiments, who, putting aside all fear of the present situation, organized a private committee with the exclusive end of aiding materially and morally the reconcentrados. This neither has been nor is at present an easy task. The great number of the poor and scarcity of means make us encounter constant conflicts. This conflict is more terrible with the official elements and in a special manner with the mayor of the city and the civil authorities, who try by all means to annihilate this good work. The result of the collections are very insignificant if we bear in mind the thousands of people who suffer from the reconcentrations; but it serves for some consolation to see that in Havana some 159 children and 84 women are well cared for in the asylum erected in Cadiz street, No. 82, and 93 women and children are equally well located in a large saloon erected for them in the second story of the fosos, with good food and proper medical assistance, as also everything indispensable to civilized life.

According to the information which we have been able to acquire since August until the present day, 1,700 persons have entered the Fosos proceeding from Jaruco, Campo Florido, Guanabo, and Tapaste, in the province of Havana. Of these, only 243 are living now and are to be found in Cadiz street—82 in the saloon already mentioned and 61 in the Quinta del Rey and the Hospital Mercedes, the whole amounting to about 397, and of these a great many will die on account of the great sufferings and hunger they have gone through.

From all this we deduct that the number of deaths among the reconcentrados has amounted to 77 per cent.

Mr. Lee to Mr. Day.

No. 717.] UNITED STATES CONSULATE-GENERAL,
Havana, December 3, 1897.

SIR: Referring to my cipher telegram of the 1st instant, which I beg to confirm, reading as follows:

ASSISTANT SECRETARY OF STATE, etc.:

Inform the Department that he has learned from the United States consul at Matanzas of an extensive and dangerous conspiracy, under the ex-governor of the province, directed against Americans, action against them to be contingent upon movement of the United States Government in favor of independence to Cuba.

I have the honor to state that rumors have been more or less frequent regarding the riotous intentions of some of the dissatisfied elements toward citizens of the United States dwelling here and in other parts of the island. Any riotous demonstrations here must come from the Spanish noncombatants or from the volunteer forces. I do not think there is any danger from the former, many of whom seem to be in favor of annexation, rather than for real autonomy or for an independent Cuban Republic. And I am inclined to think if General Blanco can manage the volunteers as yesterday he said he could, the trouble from that source is diminishing. The origin of the mobs in this city in the past has always been located in the ranks of the volunteers, who alone have organization and arms.

The Governor and Captain-General is now investigating the Matanzas rumors and will, I am sure, deal promptly with any conspirators found there.

The Weyler police have all been changed and the officers of the volunteers, too, when the Government here has reason to doubt their loyalty.

In consequence of all this, and the assurances of the governmental authorities that American life and property will, if necessary, be protected by them at a moment's notice, I have declined to make an application for the presence of one or more war ships in this harbor, and have advised those of our people who have wives and children here not to send them away, at least for the present, because such proceedings would not, in my opinion, be justifiable at this time, from the standpoint of personal security.

I still think that two war ships at least should be at Key West, prepared to move here at short notice, and that more of them should be sent to Dry Tortugas, and a coal station be established there. Such proceedings would seem to be in line with that prudence and foresight necessary to afford safety to the Americans residing on the island, and to their properties, both of which, I have every reason to know, are objects of the greatest concern to our Government.

I am, etc.,

FITZHUGH LEE,
Consul-General.

Mr. Lee to Mr. Day.

No. 718.]   UNITED STATES CONSULATE-GENERAL,
Havana, December 3, 1897.

SIR: I have the honor to state that a representative of a Madrid paper here says that:

Canalejas has said, upon his return from the Vuelta Abajo, or Pinar del Rio province, after the recent combat there between the Spanish generals Bernal and Hernandez de Valasco, in command of 2,300 men, and two pieces of artillery, and Cuban forces under Pedro Diaz, that although the Spanish troops have displayed once more their usual valor in the said fight, and the enemy must have suffered heavy losses, yet the province of Pinar del Rio is not pacified, and that there are numerous rebel forces still there. That out of about 14,000 Spanish regular troops in that province, only about 3,000 or 4,000 are able to operate, the balance being sick at the hospitals, garrisoning towns, and otherwise distributed. That he believes autonomy premature, and inclines himself to the adoption of energetic military action for the purpose of finally pacifying said province. That he does not believe in altering facts and news. That the truth, no matter how painful and bitter it may be, must be known in the peninsula, where public opinion and the press has been deceived regarding the annihilation of the war and the so-called pacification of the western provinces, among which that of Pinar del Rio has been included.

The Lucha to-day publishes that Canalejas has said "that the economic condition of the Pinar del Rio province is deplorable, there being 40,000 reconcentrados absolutely destitute, 15,000 of which are children, most of whom are orphans; that they are unequally distributed throughout the different towns in the province, there being only 460 at the capital, city of Pinar del Rio, while in small towns like Consolacioa and Candelaria there are over 4,000. The municipalities can not incur any expense, because the taxes can not be collected, because most of the taxpayers, if not all, have been ruined by the war."

I am, etc.,

FITZHUGH LEE,
Consul-General.

Mr. Lee to Mr. Day.

No. 723.]   UNITED STATES CONSULATE-GENERAL,
                    Havana, December 7, 1897.
SIR:
* * * * * * *

(The consul-general informs the Assistant Secretary of State that measures for the relief of the reconcentrados are not sufficiently energetic to be effective, and that he is advised by the Governor-General that authority to admit articles of food and clothing from the United States to Cuban ports free of duty rested with the authorities at Madrid.)

I see no effects of the governmental distribution to the reconcentrados. I am informed that only $12,500, in Spanish silver, had been dedicated to the Havana province out of the $100,000 said to have been set aside for the purpose of relieving them on the island, and that reports from all parts of the province show that 50 per cent have already died and that many of those left will die. Most of these are women and children. I do not believe the Government here is really able to relieve the distress and sufferings of these people.

* * * * * * *

I am informed an order has been issued in some parts of the island suspending the distribution of rations to reconcentrados. * * * The condition of these people is simply terrible.

I inclose herewith an official copy of the comparative mortality in Havana for the six months ending November 30. It will be perceived that there has been a great increase in the death rate, and without adequate means in the future to prevent it the mortality will increase. I hear of much suffering in the Spanish hospitals for want of food and among the Spanish soldiers. * * * I hear, also, that the Spanish merchants in some parts of the island are placing their establishments in the names of foreigners in order to avoid their provisions being purchased on credit by the military administration, and that the Spanish army is suffering much from sickness and famine, and that a great deal of money is needed at once to relieve their condition. In some parts of the island, I am told, there is scarcely any food for soldiers or citizens, and that even cats are used for food purposes, selling at 30 cents apiece.

It is a fair inference therefore to draw from the existing conditions, that it is not possible for the Governor-General of this island to relieve the present situation with the means at his disposal. * * *

I am, etc.,
                    FITZHUGH LEE,
                         Consul-General.

[Confidential.]
Mr. Lee to Mr. Day.

No. 726.]   UNITED STATES CONSULATE-GENERAL,
         Havana, December 13, 1897. (Received December 18.)
SIR: I have the honor to make the following report:
* * * * * * *

The contest for and against autonomy is most unequal. For it, there are five or six of the head officers at the palace, and twenty or thirty other persons here in the city.

Against it, first, are the insurgents, with or without arms, and the Cuban noncombatants; second, the great mass of the Spaniards, bearing or nonbearing arms—the latter desiring, if there must be a change, annexation to the United States.

Indeed, there is the greatest apathy concerning autonomy in any form. No one asks what it will be, or when, or how it will come.

I do not see how it could be even put into operation by force, because, as long as the insurgents decline to accept it, so long, the Spanish authorities say, the war must continue.

* * * * * * *

I am obliged to say, too, that * * * the Government of this island has not been able to relieve from starvation the Cuban population driven from their homes by the Weyler edict, and no longer attempts to do so.

I am, etc.,
FITZHUGH LEE,
Consul-General.

Mr. Lee to Mr. Day.

No. 727.]   UNITED STATES CONSULATE-GENERAL,
Havana, December 14, 1897.

SIR: I have the honor to report that I have received information that in the province of Havana reports show that there have been 101,000 "reconcentrados," and that out of that 52,000 have died. Of the said 101,000, 32,000 were children. This excludes the city of Havana and seven other towns from which reports have not yet been made up. It is thought that the total number of reconcentrados in Havana province will amount to 150,000, nearly all women and children, and that the death rate among their whole number from starvation alone will be over 50 per cent.

For the above number of reconcentrados $12,500, Spanish silver, was set aside out of the $100,000 appropriated for the purpose of relieving all the reconcentrados on the island. Seventy-five thousand of the 150,000 may be still living, so if every dollar appropriated of the $12,500 reaches them the distribution will average about 17 cents to a person, which, of course, will be rapidly exhausted, and as I can hear of no further succor being afforded, it is easy to perceive what little practical relief has taken place in the condition of those poor people.

I am, etc.,
FITZHUGH LEE.

Mr. Lee to Mr. Day.

No. 732.]   UNITED STATES CONSULATE-GENERAL,
Havana, December 28, 1897.

SIR: I have the honor to report that I have been informed by the authorities here that they are now engaged in forming an autonomistic cabinet and arranging for the members to take the required oath on the 1st January next, and also for an election to take place thirty days thereafter.

* * * * * * *

My present information is that most of the Spaniards will refrain from voting, and nearly all of the Cubans.

* * * * * * *

The feeling in Havana, and I hear in other parts of the island, is strong against it—the Cubans desiring an independent republic and the Spaniards preferring annexation to the United States rather than autonomy. On the night of the 24th instant there seems to have been a concerted plan over the island to testify the disapprobation of the people to the proposed autonomistic plans of the Spanish Government. It culminated in this city about 2 o'clock in the morning of the 25th, in the principal square of Havana, where a mob assembled with cries of "Death to autonomy!" and to General Blanco, and shouting " Viva Weyler!" These men came to the square with stones in their pockets, and some of them armed with weapons.

They made a demonstration, too, against the office of the Diario de la Marina, a paper published in this town favoring autonomy, but were dispersed by the military police and soldiers.

* * * * * * *

I am, etc.,

FITZHUGH LEE.

Mr. Lee to Mr. Day.

No. 733.] UNITED STATES CONSULATE-GENERAL,
Havana, December 28, 1897.

SIR: I have the honor to acknowledge receipt of the following telegrams:

WASHINGTON, *December 24.*

LEE, *Consul-General, Havana:*

The following was given to the public, in pursuance of an arrangement this day made with the Spanish minister to that effect: "By direction of the President, the public is informed that in deference to the earnest desire of the Government to contribute by effective action toward the relief of the suffering people in the Island of Cuba, arrangements have been perfected, by which charitable contributions in money or kind can be sent to the island by the benevolently disposed people of the United States. Money, provisions, clothing, medicines, and the like articles of prime necessity can be forwarded to General Fitzhugh Lee, the consul-general of the United States at Havana, and all articles now dutiable by law so consigned will be admitted into Cuba free of duty.

The consul-general has been instructed to cooperate with the local authorities and the charitable boards for the distribution of such relief among the destitute and needy people of Cuba. The President is confident that the people of the United States, who have on many occasions in the past responded most generously to the cry for bread from people stricken by famine or sore calamity, and who have beheld no less generous action on the part of foreign communities, when their own countrymen have suffered from fire and flood, will heed the appeal for aid that comes from the destitute at their threshold, and especially at this season of good will and rejoicing, give of their abundance to this humane end.—John Sherman." Please cooperate with the local authorities to this end.

DAY.

WASHINGTON, *December 27.*

LEE, *Consul-General, Havana:*

Wire immediately character of supplies most needed for Cuban relief. Will money be of more service than food, clothing, etc.?

DAY.

I have also the honor to confirm the following telegram:

HAVANA, *December 27.*

ASSISTANT SECRETARY OF STATE, *Washington:*

Summer clothing, second-hand or otherwise, principally for small women and children. Medicines for fevers, a large proportion being quinine. Hard bread, corn meal, rice, lard, potatoes, beans, pease, salt fish, principally codfish, any canned goods, and especially large quantities of condensed milk, as many persons at first are too feeble for other nourishment. Money will be useful, too, to secure shelter and for nurses, attendants, and many other purposes. Think 50 per cent of the rural population have already died from starvation, the greater number being old men, women, and children.

LEE.

I am, sir, etc.,

FITZHUGH LEE,
Consul-General.

[Telegram.]

HAVANA, *January 5, 1898.*

The consul-general informs the Department that the Government of Cuba is not giving money in lieu of rations to starving people of the island.

Mr. Lee to Mr. Day.

No. 738.]
UNITED STATES CONSULATE-GENERAL,
Havana, January 5, 1898.

SIR: I have the honor to acknowledge receipt of the following cipher telegram:

WASHINGTON, *December 31.*

LEE, *Consul-General, Havana:*

Your suggestions are most timely. Arrangements are in progress to organize Red Cross receiving and forwarding bureau in New York and later probably receiving bureau in Havana, under your direction, with Red Cross agents to do detail work.

ADEE.

And to confirm the following telegram:

HAVANA, *January 1.*

ASSISTANT SECRETARY OF STATE, *Washington:*

To list add blankets and flour.

LEE.

I am, sir, etc.,

FITZHUGH LEE,
Consul-General.

Mr. Lee to Mr. Day.

No. 742.]
UNITED STATES CONSULATE-GENERAL,
Havana, January 8, 1898.

SIR: I have the honor to state, as a matter of public interest, that the "reconcentrado order" of General Weyler, formerly Governor-General of this island, transferred about 400,000 self-supporting people, principally women and children, into a multitude, to be sustained by the contributions of others or die of starvation or of fevers, resulting from a low physical condition, and being massed in large bodies, without change of clothing and without food.

Their houses were burned, their fields and plant beds destroyed, and their live stock driven away or killed.

I estimate that probably 200,000 of the rural population in the provinces of Pinar del Rio, Havana, Matanzas, and Santa Clara have died of starvation or from resultant causes, and the deaths of whole families almost simultaneously or within a few days of each other, and of mothers praying for their children to be relieved of their horrible sufferings by death, are not the least of the many pitiable scenes which were ever present. In the provinces of Puerto Principe and Santiago de Cuba, where the "reconcentrado order" could not be enforced, the great mass of the people are self-sustaining.

* * * * * * *

A daily average of 10 cents' worth of food to 200,000 people would be an expenditure of $20,000 per day, and of course the most humane efforts upon the part of our citizens can not hope to accomplish such a gigantic relief, and a great portion of these people will have to be abandoned to their fate.

* * * * * * *

I am, etc.,

FITZHUGH LEE.

Mr. Lee to Mr. Day.

No. 744.] UNITED STATES CONSULATE-GENERAL,
Havana, January 13, 1898.

SIR: I have the honor to inclose a translation of an editorial published in the Diario de la Marina of to-day.

I am, etc., FITZHUGH LEE.

[Translation.—From the Diario de la Marina, of Havana, January 13, 1898.]

Perdonalos, Senor. * * * (Forgive them, for they do not know what they are doing).

They came against the Diario.
They cried out against it.
They stoned it.
And the separatists looked on with joy.
And the *laborantes* (abettors of the rebellion), of all well known, could not restrain their rejoicing.

It was natural; what a great victory for them!

What was not accomplished by Maceo, nor Quintin Banderas, nor Maximo Gomez, was accomplished yesterday by an unconscious mob; carrying disorder, carrying riot, carrying anarchy into the heart of Havana.

And the foreign consuls witnessed the shameful spectacle from the balconies of the Hotel Inglaterra!

What shame!

Down with the Diario de la Marina! Death to the Diario de la Marina! And Maximo Gomez alive! And Calixto Garcia alive! And the assassins of the martyr Ruiz also alive!

Poor Spain!

What a difference between yesterday and to-day: Yesterday, your sons, liberals and reactionaries, fell in the streets of Madrid, fighting together the common enemy, against the oppressors of Europe, against the invincible hosts of the great Napoleon. To-day the bravery and the patriotism and the heroism consist in shouting, in outraging, and in knifing, if possible,,defenseless journalists, against whom the action of the laws of the State and in the last extreme, the laws of honor, are sufficient in any civilized country.

But what pains us the most is not this; what our hearts lament at present is not the sentiment of the honorable profession outraged; no. It is the Spanish sentiment; it is the patriotism which boils in our veins with more heat; with a hundred times more enthusiasm than in that of those —— braves, that in a mob, and in an anonymous manner, have pretended to offend us, without understanding, unfortunates, that what they have trampled on, that what they have dragged through the mud, has been the majesty of the law, the principle of authority, and the honor of the country.

What will say the representatives of foreign powers who witnessed the shameful spectacle of yesterday? What effect will this great scandal cause in the United States, where they watch our discords, where they await our errors, where they count on our folly to take possession of the apple which they have been waiting for one hundred years to ripen and thereby fall in their hands?

This, this is what pains us; this, this is what shames us; this, this is what frightens us, and not the personal danger which we may risk; if with our blood and with the sacrifice of our lives we could avoid the consequences that for our beloved country we foresee and feel as a fatal result of the sad spectacle which happened in the streets of Havana yesterday, the shedding of our blood and the sacrifice of our blood we would consider as well employed.

"This is the greatest victory which up to the present has been gained for the independence of Cuba by Maximo Gomez," was said to us by an invalid chief of the army, a veteran in the past insurrection and of the African war, who came to the Diario de la Marina as soon as he received notice of the uprising.

Yes, a victory for Maximo Gomez and a day of rejoicing for the enemies of Spain. This is what signifies, before all and above all, the seditions tumult of yesterday.

Mr. Lee to Mr. Day.

No. 746.]
UNITED STATES CONSULATE GENERAL,
Havana, January 13, 1898.

SIR: I have the honor to transmit herewith some statistics sent me about the mortality in the town of Santa Clara, the capital of Santa Clara province, situated about 33 miles south of Sagua, which numbers some 14,000 inhabitants. It will be noticed that there were 5,489 deaths in that town in the seven years previous to 1897, which included 1,417 in one year, from an epidemic of yellow fever, while in 1897, owing to the concentration order, there were 6,981; the concentration order went into effect in February.

In that year, 1897, the month's death rate for January was 78, but in February, the first month of reconcentration, there were 114, and there has been a gradual increase since, as you will see, until in December, 1897, the number of deaths was 1,011. I refer to this as a specimen of the mortality on this island in consequence of the "reconcentrado order" of the late Captain and Governor General, Weyler.

I am, etc.,
FITZHUGH LEE,
Consul-General.

[Inclosure in No. 746.]

STATISTICS OF DEATH RATE IN SANTA CLARA.

(A town of 14,000 inhabitants.)

1890	578	1896 (epidemic of yellow fever among army and Cubans)	1,417
1891	720		
1892	596		
1893	619		5,489
1894	687	1897 (no epidemic)	6,981
1895	872		

(1,492 more than in seven previous years.)

CUBAN CORRESPONDENCE. 19

Concentration order in February, 1897—Monthly death rate.

January	78	August	645
February (concentration)	114	September	630
March	333	October	884
April	524	November	1,037
May	539	December	1,011
June	531		
July	655	Total	6,981

Sample month, December, 1897.

	Number of deaths.	Number of patients.
Civil Hospital	143	170
Military Hospital	23	700
San Lazarus Hospital	2	10
Buried in poor carts	228	
Buried by family	553	
Prison	2	
Total	951	

Mr. Lee to Mr. Day.

No. 747.]
UNITED STATES CONSULATE-GENERAL,
Havana, January 15, 1898.

SIR: I have the honor to confirm the following cipher telegram to you:

HAVANA, *January 12.*

Spanish officers with a mob at their heels make an attack upon four autonomist newspapers. The rioting continued until 1 p. m.

HAVANA, *January 12.*

Apprehend serious disturbances as consequence of intense prevailing excitement. Antiautonomists began trouble, confining their attacks to autonomists. Rioting ceased, but many rumors. Consulate-general and palace heavily guarded.

HAVANA, *January 13.*

Reports condition of affairs quiet. City under guard. Mobs yesterday cried, Death to autonomy and Blanco, and long live Weyler. The conflict is between Spanish factions. Some of the rioters proposed going to United States consulate. Ships not needed now, but may be later.

HAVANA, *January 13.*

Spanish officers and mob attacked three newspaper offices, not four (as reported yesterday). Soldiers joined the mob when sent to defend the newspapers, and outside the palace shouted death to Blanco and autonomy. If Americans are in danger ships should be ready to move promptly for Havana. Uncertainty and excitement widespread.

HAVANA, *January 14.*

A few casualties. Disorder last night and this morning and crowds shouting death to Blanco and autonomy. Fears nothing very grave at present.

HAVANA.

(Noon. All quiet.)

HAVANA, *January 15.*

Quiet prevails.

I have also the honor to acknowledge the receipt of the following cipher telegram, received yesterday from you:

WASHINGTON, *January 14.*

LEE, *Consul-General, Havana:*

(Instructs him to maintain frequent communication with United States squadron in Key West as to state of affairs at Havana. He should also frequently advise the Department of the situation.)

I am, etc.,

FITZHUGH LEE.

Mr. Lee to Mr. Day.

[Confidential.]

No. 749.] UNITED STATES CONSULATE-GENERAL.
Havana, January 18, 1898. (Received January 22.)

SIR: The recent disorders in this city are to be primarily attributed to a group of Spanish officers who were incensed at articles appearing in three of the newspapers of Havana, El Reconcentrado, La Discusion, and El Diario de la Marina. The first was very pronounced against General Weyler and his methods, the Discusion had been suppressed by Weyler, but its publication was permitted to be resumed by Blanco, and the last had been an ultra Spanish organ, but had been converted by the present authorities to autonomy.

It is probable that the Spanish officers were first provoked by the denunciations of Weyler in the columns of one of these papers and determined to stop it, and afterwards, being supported by the mob, turned the demonstration into an antiautonomistic affair.

* * * * * * *

I send to-day an analysis of the autonomistic plan. The intense opposition to it on the part of the Spaniards arises from the fact that the the first appointment of officers to put into form its provisions were made generally outside of their party in order to show the Cubans in arms that autonomy was instituted for their benefit and protection.

* * * * * * *

The intelligent Spaniards * * * see no prosperity in the future, but rather other wars and more confusion in the same old attempts to make the waters of commerce flow in unnatural channels. The lower Spanish classes have nothing in mind when autonomy is mentioned except Cuban local rule; hence their opposition.

* * * * * * *

I am, etc.,

FITZHUGH LEE,
Consul-General.

P. S.—The paper referred to will go by the next steamer.

Mr. Lee to Mr. Day.

No. 754.] UNITED STATES CONSULATE-GENERAL,
Havana, January 21, 1898. (Received January 25.)

SIR:

* * * * * * *

I have the honor to transmit herewith a document containing "Observations regarding the decree which established on the Island of Cuba the autonomic régime," and two copies of the Havana Gazette containing the decree referred to.

I am, etc.,

FITZHUGH LEE,
Consul-General.

[Inclosure No. 1, with dispatch No. 754. Translation.]

OBSERVATIONS REGARDING THE DECREE WHICH ESTABLISHES ON THE ISLAND OF CUBA THE AUTONOMIC RÉGIME.

1. Article 3 grants to the insular chambers, together with the Governor-General, the power to legislate regarding colonial affairs "in the form and terms designated

by law." What law? Those decreed by the Cortes at Madrid? It appears so, because the provisions of a general character emanating from the said Cortes shall receive the name of laws, while the colonial legislative provisions shall be called statutes. And if the Cortes of the Kingdom is the one to fix the form and terms of the colonial resolutions, it has a powerful arm in its hands and can annul the action of the insular chambers.

2. The insular representation is composed of two bodies, with the same authority—the chamber of representatives and the council of administration. Article 4 provides that the chamber is formed by popular election; but that concession, which at first seems extensive, when examined in its relations with the other powers given to the insular representation, is practically deficient. No colonial resolution can be in force unless it has been approved by the chamber and the council. The council, as we shall see later, from the nature of its composition, will be controlled by the Government in such a manner that the representatives of the people to the chamber will always find themselves in the power of the Government in some way. They will not be able to do anything, because if the council does not approve, or should modify the decision of the other house—the chamber—the latter's decisions will have no effect. The veto granted by article 43 will not be required.

3. The council of administration is composed of 25 members; 17 are appointed directly by the Government; the remaining 18 are elected by popular vote. To be elected a member of said council it is necessary to be a Spaniard (Spanish subject), 35 years of age, and possessing an income of $4,000 for two years previous to election. The formation of the council will be therefore controlled by the Government, because the Government will appoint unconditionally the 17 members, and it will be very easy for the Government to find one or more votes among those owing their election to the people, the more so as the conditions required to be a councilor are favorable to those near the Government. In order to pass any measure the presence of a majority of those composing this legislative body is required. It will be very difficult to have all the 18 members elected by the people vote as a unit, and the absence of one or two will be sufficient to give the governmental members control of the body, or the vote be a tie.

If the members elected should stand together on any measure objectionable to the Government, they could be sent to their homes by the Governor-General, and he can instruct or direct the election of others more accommodating. On the other hand, the members by governmental appointment can not be removed—their offices or positions cease with their lives. The Governor-General can not remove them. And to this end they will be carefully selected as faithful instruments of the Government, in whose hands the whole autonomistic machine will be placed. It is known that in Canada all senators are appointed by the Government; but it should be remembered that the Governor-General appoints them, with the advice and consent of its counselors or ministers, and that these counselors are elected by the parliament, and the parliament by the people, the result is, that in Canada the senators are representatives of the people, while here in Cuba the Government can control them.

4. As if the authority to veto was not sufficient (art. 43) and the power did not exist to suspend, close the sessions, and adjourn both bodies, or either of them, by the decree of the Governor-General, article 30 grants more authority or power to present [prevent?] or annul the freedom or liberty of the discussions of the colonial parliament, when, in the opinion of the Governor-General, the national interests will be affected by a colonial statute. The bill in question can not even be discussed unless previously authorized by the central government, and it is a limitation or restriction which has no precedent in any known autonomistic legislation. It is improper because the restriction arises before the debates show the character of the measure to be discussed. It reveals, besides, a mistrust or want of confidence of the mere discussion of the subject.

A Governor-General may decree that all bills or colonial statutes may be, in his opinion, contrary to the national interest, and that nothing should be discussed in the local legislative bodies without the previous consent of the Madrid Government. All guaranties are for the Madrid power; there are none for the colony, except the one named in article 43, which fixes the limit within which the Madrid Government has to decide regarding the right of a veto which a colonial statute may have received from the Governor-General.

5. Article 36 grants exclusive power to the Cortes of the Kingdom to determine the expenses of sovereignty which the colony has to pay and the necessary receipts to cover them, for the Cortes can alter them at pleasure. Therefore the colony has no direct vote in a matter of so great importance. It may be said that she is allowed to appoint her deputies to the Cortes of the Kingdom, and that through them the colony can be heard. But the colony's voice will be lost, because their number would be insignificant before the remaining deputies of the nation. And it may happen that the expenses of sovereignty, put by the Cortes on the colony, absorb all of its receipts, because neither of the two houses (chambers) can delib-

erate regarding the colonial budget without having first voted to pay the expenses of sovereignty.

6. Article 37 speaks of treaties of commerce which may affect Cuba, and states that the Madrid Government shall make them, aided by the delegates of the colonial government. And, further, that when the treaties are approved by the Cortes of the Kingdom they will be published as general laws, and as such will be respected in the insular territory, but it is left doubtful whether they would be laws in Cuba if the colonial delegates should reject them. If the Madrid Government is not to rule in such a case it should be so stated. And if it is a law notwithstanding the colonial opposition, why is the concurrence of the colony asked? The case referred to in article 38 does not decide it, because it only refers to those treaties in the negotiation of which the insular government has had nothing to do.

7. Article 40 gives in a very ingenious manner a method of deciding the differences arising from privileged articles of commerce, in comparison to similar foreign articles, and in reference to the extension of such a privilege, within the maximum limit of 35 per cent differential duty. When the two governments making the treaty do not agree, a committee is formed of the same number of Cuban and peninsular deputies. These deputies appoint their president; if they do not agree, the oldest in age presides. And the president has the casting vote. Let us suppose the Cuban deputies to be very patriotic, which is, by the way, supposing a great deal, but as they will never be more patriotic than the peninsular delegates, it will result that they will not agree, and then the oldest will decide. As there are a large number of peninsular deputies and a very small number of insular deputies to select from, care will be taken that some aged peninsular deputy be appointed on said committee, and he would be the one to decide. The matter would have been simplified by stating that the eldest peninsular deputy would be the one to make the lists, as such will be the result.

8. Article 40 also refers to the schedules of the merchandise, which will appear in the privileged lists. The decree only says that they shall be made by mutual consent (meaning Cuban and Peninsular deputies). It does not make any reference to the case when there is no mutual consent, which makes us suppose that the same procedure recommended in the other lists will be observed. The eldest Peninsular deputy will therefore make the said schedules.

9. The Governor-General has the power to suspend the constitutional guarantees, apply legislation of public order (ley de órden público), and adopt any measures he may deem fit to maintain peace, etc. This power the Governor-General can exercise at will, without any limitation, because he is not obliged to hear the opinion of the council of secretaries (ministry), and thus the whole political system of the country lies with the Governor-General. The latter can therefore find any pretext for courts martial, the application of the code of military justice, and all that series of proclamations and orders which have caused so much harm, and which rob the citizen of all guarantees and protection.

10. The distribution of the public debt of Cuba remains completely in the hands and subject to the decision of the Cortes of the Kingdom, which will try to assign to Cuba as much of it as it can, so that Spain will pay the smallest part.

Beyond all this, even, the fact remains and makes useless, while it exists, all orderly and pacific development of the autonomistic régime, and this fact is the existence of the volunteers in arms. The political party in power is unarmed, has no force of its own, while the Spanish radical (intransigente) party, which is in the opposition, is armed, having on its side the armed volunteers. Under such conditions there can be no genuine autonomistic government, because the opposition can ride over, whenever it pleases, the authority of the local government, and of which we had a very recent example, and it can have it repeated whenever the radical Spanish (intransigente) party so desire.

Mr. Lee to Mr. Day.

No. 756.] UNITED STATES CONSULATE GENERAL,
Havana, January 22, 1898.

SIR: I have the honor to acknowledge receipt of the following telegrams from you:

WASHINGTON, *January 17.*

Instructs consul-general to report concerning rumor that the landing of supplies from the *Vigilancia* for the Cuban sufferers was being obstructed by customs authorities, and to prevent such delays, if likely to occur.

And I beg to confirm the following telegrams to you:

HAVANA, *January 15.*
(All quiet.)

HAVANA, *January 16.*
All quiet.

HAVANA, *January 17.*
(Reports supplies by Carcho a week since delivered to-day. Regulations and recent rioting causes of delay. Apprehends no difficulty as to landing supplies and reports arrival to-day of *Vigilancia.*)

HAVANA, *January 18.*
All tranquil.

HAVANA, *January 19.*
Reports that November 4 decree admitting cattle into Cuba free until January 10 is extended to March 10 of present year, with conditions unchanged, and adds that quiet prevails.

HAVANA, *January 21.*
All quiet.

HAVANA, *January 22.*
(Reports no foreign naval vessels at Havana, but that two such German ships are expected to arrive during January.)

I am, etc.,

FITZHUGH LEE.

Mr. Lee to Mr. Day.

No. 767.]   UNITED STATES CONSULATE-GENERAL,
Havana, February 1, 1898.

SIR: I have the honor to report that I have received $1,743.46 from various sections of the country, in addition to the $5,000 first sent, making a total of $6,743.46, which have been placed to the credit or the unofficial fund. Of this amount about $3,000 have been already expended in purchasing food, paying railroad freights on provisions sent away from the city, and the salary and expenses of an agent to attend to the purchase and distribution, who acts with the committee appointed by the government of the city. It will be necessary to keep sufficient funds on hand to meet the expenses necessarily incurred in the work here.

Most of the money I have received has been in small sums, the $1,743.46 being contributed by 37 different persons. Last mail brought me $200 from an unknown donor in Baltimore, Md. I do not see any diminution in the numbers of the suffering poor on this island, except by the daily deaths occurring everywhere from starvation. The present population, which has been concentrated at various places under Weyler's proclamation is still there, not daring to go out to their homes in the interior, if said homes were still in existence, so they continue to herd together with no employment and with but little means of subsistence outside of what we are now trying to afford them. The condition of the reconcentrados is worse in the vicinity of the smaller towns, because they can get something by begging in the larger ones, and hence the death rate is greater in the small towns.

The fact that the greater majority of these poor people are principally women and children makes the sad story of suffering and death more heartrending.

I am, sir, etc.,   FITZHUGH LEE,
Consul-General.

Mr. Lee to Mr. Day.

No. 773.]   UNITED STATES CONSULATE-GENERAL,
             Havana, February 10, 1898. (Received February 15.)

SIR: I have the honor to inclose herewith a statement of the condition of some of the small towns in the neighborhood of this city. These reports are made to me by a person I sent to those places for the purpose of ascertaining the numbers and condition of the destitute and starving people in and about said towns. His name is not signed to the report for obvious reasons.

I am, etc.,
                                   FITZHUGH LEE,
                                   Consul-General.

[Inclosure in No. 773.]

MELENA DEL SUR.

The unhealthy conditions of this town and the total want of resources make it completely impossible for the mayor to remedy the present miserable situation of the people, who die in great numbers from starvation, fever, and smallpox, which is vastly spreading, owing to the lack of vaccination virus or the necessary funds to acquire it with.

There are other towns in the same conditions, as, for example, Guines, Catalina, and Madruga, whose situation could be, in a small degree, relieved if the country people were allowed to leave the town freely in search of food, which is very scarce. In some towns this is entirely prohibited; in others they are obliged to pay a tax, and, not having anything to eat, how can they pay a tax? In every town you visit the first thing you notice is the unhealthy condition of the men, and their total want of physical strength, which prevents them even from making an effort to procure the means of support.

CATALINE DE GÜINES.

The condition of the reconcentrados in this town is very sad and desperate. There are no "zones for cultivation," and they are therefore not allowed even with a military pass to leave the town in search of work or food, which latter is so scarce that one must walk 4 or 5 miles before finding a sweet potato. Among these poor there are many who have not even the meanest hut for a dwelling place and who find nobody willing to help them in the least thing.

In these districts the liberty given by General Blanco to the reconcentrados is a farce.

GÜINES TOWN.

The land near the town which comprises the "zone for cultivation" has been rented by four Spaniards, who have done this by means of their wealth and influence in the present situation. They employ the few reconcentrados who are able to work, paying them 30 or 40 cents a day. Nobody can leave the town in search of work without a pass from the military commander, which pass is good for a month only and costs 20 cents. These workmen have to leave the town at 6 in the morning, and not being able to take the meals with them, are obliged to work until 6 in the evening without any nourishment. The same thing happens to all those who go in search of food. The women who leave the town in search of vegetables, even on their own farms, which are now completely abandoned, are sometimes deprived of them on their way back by the guerrillas.

In fifteen days 200 reconcentrados have died in Guines from starvation and total lack of resources. Many of the sick sleep on the floor and in the piazzas.

One of the few real protectors of the reconcentrados, in fact a heroic one, is a young man named José Amohedo, whose father and mother have died attending to the suffering poor, and who himself has given up eight houses that belonged to him as dwelling places for the reconcentrados, all the contents of a grocery store that he possessed, and who is actually as destitute as they are, but always attending to those who suffer.

[Telegram.]

General Lee to Mr. Day.

HAVANA, *February 10, 1898.*

Captain-General returned yesterday; met with no success of any sort. Spaniards everywhere unfriendly; rumors of coming demonstration against him here. I think him excellent man, but in unfortunate position. Three serious combats reported within a week; in each insurgents victorious.

Mr. Lee to Mr. Day.

[Confidential.]

No. 775.] UNITED STATES CONSULATE-GENERAL,
Havana, February 15, 1898.

SIR: I have the honor to transmit herewith a letter, with its translation, signed by the insurgent commander in chief and addressed to the President of the United States. The said letter was delivered by a messenger, who at once departed, before I saw or had any communication with him.

I am, etc.

FITZHUGH LEE,
Consul-General.

[Inclosure in No. 775.—Translation.]

WILLIAM MCKINLEY,
President of the United States.

SIR: The heroic Cuban people possesses, as a characteristic quality of its moral being and developed to a high degree, one of the most noble sentiments, namely, gratitude; whoever has done well for Cuba wins for himself forever the lively recognition of the sons of Cuba's soil.

Your great people have given to the whole world an example of lofty virtue, and to the shame and stain of Spain, not only has it shown compassion before the great misfortunes brought on Cuba by the ferocious Spanish policy, but has extended a helping hand to the unhappy victims of the warfare carried on by the army of that nation.

The gratitude of this people must be on a par with that great and generous impulse, and if Cuba, by its geographical position and the necessity of its commercial existence, is called to maintain, once that it is free, and for the mutual benefit of both countries, closer relations with your great republic than with any other nation whatever, from this day forward Cuba will consider herself bound by a closer tie in the affection it bears for the noble American magnanimity.

However true and minute may be the reports that you have heard, never will you be able to form a just conception of all the bloodshed, the misery, the ruin and the sorrow caused to afflicted Cuba, to obtain her independence, and how the despotic spirit of Spain, irritated to the last degree before the most just of all rebellions, has revelled in the most implacable destruction of everything, lives and property. The nation which at one time accepted the inquisition and invented its tortures lastly conceived the concentration scheme, the most horrible of all means, first to martyrize and then to annihilate an entire people, and if it has stopped in the path of destruction it is due in great measure to the cry of indignation which the knowledge of such horrors unanimously drew from the States over which you govern.

The people who are saved from extinction and whose evils your gifts assuage are the people for whose liberty we daily shed our blood on the fields of battle; the country whose independence we now conquer at the point of the sword for them is also for us; blood of our blood and flesh of our flesh, we must rejoice with them in their joys as we weep and sympathize with them in their sorrows and grief.

Be not surprised, then, that as the general in chief of this Cuban army I am so deeply moved at the wave of compassion which agitates your noble country, and that I accede to the requests of the patriots I command to appear before you, the representative of the great nation, as the exponent of our immense gratitude.

I have, therefore, sir, to fulfill a conscientious duty by setting forth a fact, which I beg you will please transmit to the knowledge of the persons to whom is recommended the philanthropic mission of succoring the unhappy destitute Cubans, and in order that ignorance of certain antecedents may not deprive many needy ones of the enjoyment of that noble American charity.

The revolution, as absolute master of the country, has never prohibited any citizen, whatever his nationality, from earning his living, and it has happened that as soon as the barbarous concentration decree was derogated innumerable families have left and still leave the city for the field, impelled by hunger to wrest from the fruitful Cuban vegetation the means of relieving the most pressing needs of life. Those unhappy beings ignore the fact that if the Spaniards, by steel and privation, have shrouded their hearths in mourning, so also it might be said that the flora of Cuba was in mourning, devastated by the bullet and torch.

Wherefore, being in the same circumstances, those unfortunates have the same moral right to participate in the relief furnished to needed Cubans by your generous people. Many a widow, many a mother, many an orphan do we meet in our way who asks of us succor that we are not able to give but most sparingly, and therefore upon pointing out to them the charity awakened in their behalf in your noble nation, I desire to honor myself by offering my services to cooperate in the noble work with all the power and means within the reach of the forces I command.

I am, sir, with the most distinguished consideration,

M. GOMEZ.

Mr. Lee to Mr. Day.

No. 785.] UNITED STATES CONSULATE-GENERAL,
Havana, March 1, 1898.

SIR: I have the honor to report that the distribution of food, medicines, and clothing to the destitute on this island is satisfactorily proceeding. The work has been well organized and systematized under the immediate supervision and direction of Miss Clara Barton, president of the Red Cross Society of the United States, and her active, able, and experienced assistants.

At first the relief was confined to the city of Havana and its surrounding sections. Now that the proper organizations have been formed in the said sections the supplies have been and are being gradually extended to other portions of the island, while some of the seaports have received the necessary articles direct from New York. Of course, when the number of the poor and destitute is so large it is almost impossible to relieve large numbers in each locality, but I am able to state with confidence that under the present system of distribution the supplies are not lost or wasted, but reach those for whom they are intended.

I am, etc., FITZHUGH LEE,
Consul-General.

[Telegram.]

Mr. Lee to Mr. Day.

HAVANA, *March 3.*

Have established fine asylum for destitute small orphans regardless nationality. Money sent by you will be applied purchase food for said orphans.

LEE.

Mr. Lee to Mr. Day.

No. 795.] UNITED STATES CONSULATE-GENERAL,
Havana, March 11, 1898.

SIR: I am requested by Consul Barker, of Sagua, to transmit to you certain information contained in a letter received from him, and as the best means of doing so I inclose the latter without date, but received to-day.

I am, etc.,
FITZHUGH LEE,
Consul-General.

[Inclosure in No. 795.]

Mr. Barker to Mr. Lee.

DEAR SIR: I will thank you to communicate to the Department as quickly as possible the fact that the military commander and other officers of the military positively refuse to allow the reconcentrados to whom I am issuing food in its raw state to procure fuel with which to cook this food.

In addition they prohibited this class of people (I am only giving food to about one-fifth of the destitute—the authorities have quit altogether) from gathering vegetables cultivated within the protection of the forts, telling them the Americans propose to feed you, and to the Americans you must look.

Yours, very truly,
WALTER B. BARKER, Consul.

Mr. Lee to Mr. Day.

No. 797.]
UNITED STATES CONSULATE-GENERAL.
Havana, March 17, 1898.

SIR: 1 have the honor to inform the Department that by a decree dated March 5, 1898, the Governor-General has prorogued in all its parts to the 31st of March, 1899, the decree of the general government of the 19th April, 1897, relative to the suspension of legal proceedings against real estate, with the reservation, however, of what may be agreed upon in the matter by the insular chambers in due season.

I am, etc.,
FITZHUGH LEE,
Consul-General.

[Telegram.]

Mr. Lee to Mr. Day.

HAVANA, March 24, 1898.

Work of relief progressing most satisfactory. To-morrow arrangements made for 22 cars of supplies for Cienfuegos, Cardenas, Sagua, Calibarien, and Santa Clara, and other places. Railroads will carry special trains through free of charge. Have been greatly assisted by Mr. Klopsch.

LEE.

Mr. Lee to Mr. Day.

No. 803.]
UNITED STATES CONSULATE-GENERAL.
Havana, March 28, 1898.

SIR: I have honor to report that instructions have been given by the civil governor of Havana that the alcaldes and other authorities shall not give out any facts about the reconcentrados, and if any of the American relief committees should make inquiries concerning them, all such inquiries must be referred to him.

I am, etc.,
FITZHUGH LEE,
Consul-General.

Mr. Lee to Mr. Day.

No. 809.] UNITED STATES CONSULATE-GENERAL,
Havana, April 1, 1898. (Received April 5.)

SIR: With reference to the telegram I had the honor to transmit to you yesterday to the effect that the Governor-General had issued a decree terminating concentration of the country people, permitting them to return to their homes, and advising their employment on public works, I beg to inclose a translation of the articles of the decree referred to.

I am, etc.,

FITZHUGH LEE,
Consul-General.

[Inclosure No. 1 with Dispatch No. 809.]

TRANSLATION OF THE ARTICLES OF GENERAL BLANCO'S PROCLAMATION OF THE 30TH MARCH, 1898, SUSPENDING THE RECONCENTRATION.

ARTICLE 1. From the publication of the present proclamation (bando) in the Gazette of Havana the reconcentration of country people throughout the island is hereby terminated, and they are authorized to return with their families to their homes, and to dedicate themselves to all kind of agricultural labors.

ART. 2. The boards of relief and all civil and military authorities shall furnish them the means, within their power, to enable the rural population to return to their former places of residence, or those which they may now select, facilitating them the aid which they may respectively dispose.

ART. 3. At the instance of the council of secretaries, and through the department of public works, the preparation and immediate realization of all public works necessary and useful to furnish work and food to the country people and their families who, through lack of means, truck farms, or want of agricultural implements, may not be able to return immediately to the fields, shall be proceeded with, as well as the establishment of soup kitchens, which may settle and cheapen such services.

ART. 4. The expenses which the compliance with this proclamation (bando) may originate, as far as they may exceed the means disposed of by the boards of relief, shall be charged to the extraordinary war credit.

ART. 5. All previous instructions issued regarding the reconcentration of the country people and all others which may be in opposition to the compliance of this proclamation are hereby derogated.

HAVANA, *March 30, 1898.*

RAMON BLANCO.

Mr. McGarr to Mr. Day.

No. 137.] CONSULATE OF THE UNITED STATES,
Cienfuegos, January 10, 1898.

SIR: All the sugar mills in this consular jurisdiction, 23 in number, have been grinding since the first of the month, and at the busy centrales the various industries incident to the gathering of the crop and the manufacture of sugar are in full and steady operation.

Several of the principal estates are owned by American citizens and corporations, and most of their skilled employees are brought from the United States.

The demand for labor on the sugar estates has drawn from the towns a great portion of the unemployed laborers and given employment to the male "concentrados," many of whom were in a state of enforced idleness and destitution. As a consequence, few of them are now seen here and the labor "congestion" has been relieved.

Small predatory parties of insurgents make frequent attempts to fire the cane fields, and it requires constant and active vigilance to prevent their destruction. The dry weather and the high winds prevailing at this season render it a simple matter for one person (who can easily conceal himself in the tall cane) to start a conflagration that will, unless promptly extinguished, destroy hundreds of acres in a few hours.

Hence the almost impossibility with the utmost watchfulness and using every practicable safeguard to prevent some loss of cane by the fires started, often under cover of darkness, by the stealthy incendiaries familiar with the locality and always on the alert for an opportunity to apply the torch.

The sugar crop is the support of all classes and especially of the laboring class, and should it be in large part destroyed a famine in reality would be inevitable.

I am, etc.,
OWEN McGARR,
United States Consul.

Mr. Brice to Mr. Day.

No. 95.] CONSULATE OF THE UNITED STATES,
Matanzas, November 17, 1897.

SIR: I have the honor to submit the following report concerning present condition of affairs in this province and city.

New civil governor, Francisco de Armas, assumed the duties of his office Thursday, 11th instant. As the autonomist * * * governor of this province, his reception was cold and informal. Spaniards, as well as Cubans, are not in sympathy with proposed autonomy and reforms. A memorial to Her Majesty, Queen Regent of Spain, extensively signed by leading Spaniards of province, asking that reform bill be not signed. This will be cabled in a day or two.

* * * * * * *

Starvation.—No relief as yet afforded the starving thousands in this province. Several days ago an order from Captain Gin was given municipal authorities to issue rations and clothing, but no attention is paid the order.

* * * * * * *

Death rate in this city over 80 persons daily, and nearly all from want of food, medicines, and clothing. As I write this a dead negro woman lies in the street, within 200 yards of this consulate, starved to death; died some time this morning, and will lie there, maybe, for days. The misery and destitution in this city and other towns in the interior are beyond description.

A general order has been issued allowing reconcentrados to return to the country, but the restrictions placed in order are such as to practically prohibit. If they went, what can they do without money, food, or shelter? Only those who can obtain employment on sugar plantations can live. Insurgents say no one will be allowed to grind in province of Matanzas. The situation is indeed deplorable, and I am free to say no real help can be expected from Spanish Government, and the fate of the remaining reconcentrados is slow, lingering death from starvation.

* * * * * * *

Insurgents are numerous and quite active the past ten days. In an engagement Saturday, 13th, near Mocha, 8 miles from this city, Spanish troops were defeated with serious loss and forced to retreat. Several sugar plantations report cane burned by insurgents, and the general opinion is little or no sugar will be made this season.

I am, etc.,
A. C. BRICE,
United States Consul.

Mr. Brice to Mr. Day.

No. 97.]
CONSULATE OF THE UNITED STATES,
Matanzas, December 17, 1897.

SIR: I have the honor to report the following Cuban news in this province, taken from personal observation and reliable sources of information:

Concentrados.—Relief offered these and other poor people by Spanish authorities is only in name. I have personally visited (on several occasions) head masters of distributing stations. Two thousand rations were given out, for a few days only, to 8,000 persons. * * * There are more than 12,000 starving people in this city to-day. One out of 4 (or 6) received the following ration: 2 ounces rice, 1½ ounces tassajo (jerked beef), and sometimes a small piece of bread, per diem. Imagine starving people being relieved by such rations! Even this ration of food has been discontinued since 11th inst. Death rate has diminished somewhat; now about 63 daily. There are less people to die.

The scenes of misery and distress daily observed are beyond belief Here is one out of hundreds. In a family of seventeen living in an old limekiln, upper part of city limits, all were found dead except three, and they barely alive. * * * A few of the strongest of these people have been sent out to sugar plantations, which expect to grind. They get 30 cents per day and board themselves. General Blanco's order, allowing reconcentrados, owners of plantations and farms, to return and cultivate crops, etc., is inoperative and of no avail. Several of our American citizens, owners of land, have repeatedly asked the civil governor of this province for permission to return to their homes, and in every case refused or restrictions imposed making it impossible to comply with.

* * * * * * *

A few plantations are grinding cane. In every case they are heavily guarded by Spanish troops, and have paid insurgents for so doing. Was shown a letter from insurgent chief to owner of a large plantation, in which price demanded for grinding was 2,000 centones ($10,600 United States gold). It was paid. To make crop of sugar this season money, oxen, and laborers must be had.

* * * *

I am, etc.,
A. C. BRICE,
United States Consul.

Mr. Brice to Mr. Day.

No. 99.]
CONSULATE OF THE UNITED STATES,
Matanzas, January 18, 1898.

SIR: I have the honor to report the following concerning destitute American citizens, Matanzas province:

* * * * * * *

Up to Sunday, January 9, 1898, weekly rations of food have been regularly issued, also medicines for sick, and, although there has been more or less hardships and suffering for want of clothing, shelter, etc. (which we were not allowed to supply), none of our people have suffered for food or medicine.

* * * * * * *

In behalf of these people, I earnestly ask the Department that some prompt measures be taken to further relieve them. They are absolutely helpless—no work, shut up in cities and towns like rats in a trap to starve. We have fifteen or eighteen families (American reconcentrados) who own property in the country, and were they allowed to go to their homes, could make a good living. All these have begged and pleaded with authorities (under Blanco's order) to go, and in every case refused.

Since the 24th of May, 1897, to December 26, 1897, seven months, we have given food and medicines and relief to an average of 305 persons, American citizens, at a cost of $8,175.48 Spanish gold. This amount received from Havana on account of Cuban relief fund to date. We require a little over $800 (bills not rendered) to settle last two weeks' ration bills and three weeks' medicine.

* * * * * * *

I am, etc.,
A. C. BRICE,
United States Consul.

[Inclosure in No 99.]

CUBAN DESTITUTION.

Circular letter dated January 8, 1898, from Department of State, received yesterday.

This intimates that help is to be extended by the United States to the starving people in Cuba. The news of this relief has been known for the past two weeks and has extended all over the province. This consulate has been overwhelmed with people of all classes asking to be remembered when this relief comes.

I submit a few facts illustrating the suffering in this province alone. There are in Matanzas Province over 90,000 people who are in actual starving condition and require food, clothing, and medicines.

In addition to above, there are thousands of families (of the better classes, formerly well to do) who to-day are living on one meal a day, and that very scant. They have sold or pawned furniture, jewelry, clothing, etc., to eke out an existence until all is gone, or nearly so. Too proud to beg, they suffer in silence, and many die of starvation. The daughter of a former governor of this province was seen begging on the streets (incognito) of this city. Many of these people call on me privately at my residence asking and praying for God's sake to be remembered when this relief comes from the United States. One has to be here, know and mingle with these people, to fully realize the terrible destitution and misery existing in Cuba. It is to be hoped that this relief from the United States will come quickly, for hundreds are dying daily in this province of starvation. Conditions are dreadful, and no relief afforded by Spanish authorities.

I would advise that food and supplies for this province be sent direct to Matanzas, thus avoiding the railroad freight, drayage, etc. Supplies can be landed direct to warehouses (by lighters), which have been offered free of charge. The figures and facts I have stated indicate the large quantities of food and supplies required to give even temporary relief; also some cash will be required to handle and distribute supplies.

I am, etc.,
A. C. BRICE,
United States Consul.

MATANZAS, CUBA, *January 18, 1898.*

Mr. Brice to Mr. Day.

No. 100.]
CONSULATE OF THE UNITED STATES,
Matanzas, February 8, 1898.

SIR: I have the honor to inform the Department that U. S. cruiser *Montgomery* arrived in this port February 3, 1898, 10.34 a. m., leaving for Santiago de Cuba on February 5 at 6 p. m.

The usual courtesies were extended this consulate; also friendly visits from civil and military governors and other officials of province and city. Return visits made the following day, and their reception by commander and officers on board was a royal one and greatly appreciated.

The arrival of cruiser *Montgomery*, although a surprise, was hailed with delight by all classes, and sure to be productive of good results.

The striking feature was: Poor people thought vessel was bringing them food from the United States; their disappointment was great.

I am, etc.,

A. C. BRICE,
United States Consul.

Mr. Hyatt to Mr. Day.

No. 405.]   CONSULATE OF THE UNITED STATES,
Santiago de Cuba, November 15, 1897.

SIR: Since my return to Cuba I have availed myself of every opportunity possible to learn what, if any, changes have taken place during my absence.

At first I was disposed to believe that the insurgents were weakening and that the autonomists were coming to the front. Time and further investigation, however, has failed to confirm that view of the case.

The change of policy, as expressed by Captain-General Blanco, is doubtless modifying the feeling of resentment which formerly prevailed and, should the near future prove discouraging to the insurgents, would doubtless smooth the way to pacification. * * *

The promised revocation of the order of reconcentration is yet unfulfilled and beggars are very numerous. "Me estoy muriendo de hambre" (I am starving) is their most frequent salutation. Generally their appearance confirms their words.

*   *   *   *   *   *   *

What ought the United States Government do, is a question much discussed, and the answer is usually what the person desires, and sentiment, not reason, makes reply. Among property holders, whether Americans or citizens of other nationalities, there is but one sentiment. "Hands off," or such active intervention as will quickly terminate the struggle. They greatly deprecate constant agitation, which makes the governing classes enemies to American interests and brings no corresponding advantages. For your information I inclose a military order and a translation of the same, issued by the insurgent general, Calixto Garcea. General Garcea's command extends over more than half of the island, including the provinces of Porto Principe and Santiago, the portions supposed to be in most active rebellion.

Another order is issued by the same authority permitting owners of coffee estates to gather as much as they may need for family use, but none for market.

The present insurgent capital is at San Augustin Aguarris, between Holguin and Tunio, 135 miles from Santiago.

The local papers, which publish only what has been submitted to censorial examination, admit several engagements of late on those parts of the island heretofore reported as pacified.

*   *   *   *   *   *   *

I am, etc.,

PULASKI F. HYATT,
United States Consul.

CUBAN CORRESPONDENCE. 33

[Inclosure in No. 405.]

MILITARY DEPARTMENT OF THE EAST,
GENERAL HEADQUARTERS,
Baire, November 6, 1897. (Third of Independence.)

To the commanding generals of the first, second, and third army corps of eastern Cuba:

Duly informed through the press that the Spanish Government is offering autonomy with the intention by these means to subdue the revolution, or at least to bring about disturbances in our ranks and weaken our cause, this general headquarters reminds you that the spirit and letter of our constitution does not admit with Spain any treaty whatever that is not based upon the absolute independence of Cuba. In accordance with this I will be inexorable, submitting to a summary trial, and will consider as traitors all civil or military officers of whatever rank receives messages, commissions, or has any intercourse with the enemy, as the supreme government of the republic is the only one authorized, and listen to any overtures that may be made, and even the government will only listen to proposals acknowledging the absolute independence of Cuba by the Spanish Government. All persons who come within our lines commissioned by the enemy with proposals to submit to Spain will be tried and punished as spies.

In order to avoid any ignorance being professed on the subject, you will circulate this communication among your subordinates, posting this order during eight days at your headquarters and have it read in the presence of the troops.

Country and liberty.

CALIXTO GARCIA,
Commander in Chief of the Department of the East.

Baire is a small village lying about 54 miles from the city of Santiago.

Mr. Hyatt to Mr. Day.

No. 407.]
CONSULATE OF THE UNITED STATES,
Santiago de Cuba, November 20, 1897.

SIR: For the benefit of the Department of State I send the inclosed list of civil officers of the insurgent government of Cuba, elected and installed at Yaya, in the province of Porto Principe October 20.

There is rumor of renewed activity on the part of the rebels of eastern Cuba, commanded by Gen. Calixto Gracea, and the shipment of all available Spanish soldiers to Manzanillo corroborates the report.

The Spanish residents of the island are becoming very outspoken in favor of closing the war and annexation to the United States. There are numerous inquiries among them of how they can become citizens of our Government. There are also quite a number of Spanish soldiers making the same inquiry. The business Spaniards here declare that they are tired of doing business at a loss, and that peace and prosperity can only come by annexation. Many are greatly disappointed that the United States consul can not make American citizens of them at once.

With highest, etc.,

PULASKI F. HYATT,
United States Consul.

[Inclosure with No. 407.]

List of insurgent officials elected and installed at Yaya Porto Principe, Cuba, October 20, 1897:
President, Bartolo Maso.
Vice-president, Domingo Mendez, Capote.
Secretary of war, Jose B. Alerman.
Secretary of the treasury, Earnisto Font Stearling.
Secretary of foreign affairs, Andres Moreno de la Torre.
Secretary of the interior, Manuel R. Silva.
General-in-chief, Maximo Gomez.
Lieutenant-general, Calixto Gracea.

H. Doc. 406——3

Mr. Hyatt to Mr. Day.

No. 109.] CONSULATE OF THE UNITED STATES,
Santiago de Cuba, November 26, 1897.

SIR: Yesterday I cabled you as follows: "Day, Washington. All political prisoners freed. Hyatt."

This cable I now confirm. The order of release opened the doors to 12 military prisoners in Castle Morro and a somewhat larger number in the city prison, including persons of different nationalities; but no Americans, all such having been from time to time released by special orders, which is a cause of much favorable comment to our nation. * * *

The text of the new autonomy, as published here, is not meeting with favor by the most ardent friends of Spain.

* * * * * * *

There is, however, a feeling of relief and safety since the change in the captain-generalship.

Very respectfully, PULASKI F. HYATT.

Mr. Hyatt to Mr. Day.

No. 410.] CONSULATE OF THE UNITED STATES,
Santiago de Cuba, December 5, 1897.

SIR: The situation in this part of Cuba is not destitute of activity; nevertheless, it seems to be one of expectancy, both sides posing and waiting to see what will happen in the United States.

There is a more secure feeling since the arrival of Governor-General Blanco, otherwise no perceptable change. The reconcentration order is relaxed, but not removed; but many people have reached a point where it is a matter of entire indifference to them whether it is removed or not, for they have lost all interest in the problem of existence.

A census of the island taken to-day, as compared with one taken three years ago, I feel confident would show that two-thirds of the residents are missing; and the Spanish army would make no better showing.

The rainy season is practically over, and cooler weather is apparent, the thermometer ranging from 70° to 88° F. through the twenty-four hours, in the shade.

His Excellency Enrique Capriles, a former governor of this province, has returned to this post of duty. His former record is a sufficient guaranty of an honorable administration.

* * * * *

Mr. Rigney, an American sugar planter near Manzanillo, was preparing to grind during the coming season. A few nights since the insurgents fired seven cannon shots among his buildings, one ball passing through the roof of his house. Americans were hopeful that they would be allowed to make their crop, and several are making ready to do so; but the action of the insurgents toward Mr. Rigney gives the problem a doubtful aspect. It may have been a personal matter against Mr. Rigney.

The number of destitute Americans fed by this consulate decreased from 89 to 64, but is again on the increase. Since being fed, sickness among them has materially decreased and their appearance has greatly improved.

  * * * * * * *

  Very respectfully,
           PULASKI F. HYATT,
             United States Consul.

Mr. Hyatt to Mr. Day.

No. 413.]   CONSULATE OF THE UNITED STATES,
       Santiago de Cuba, December 14, 1897.

SIR: Since my last dispatch on the situation in Cuba several military engagements of more or less importance have occurred and the insurgents are claiming to have had the best in the fight; but until an engagement shall take place of sufficient importance to have a controlling influence, I can safely leave the press to report on such matters.

I take it to be a matter of far greater importance that I shall watch the trend of public opinion and its effects on the political situation, for thus far battles have not been the most important factors in the Cuban problem.

Up to the present we have only garbled accounts as to the contents of the President's message, so it is too early to say what its effects will be. I shall, however, watch such results with much concern, as all parties have looked forward to it with deepest solicitation.

The order of reconcentration is now practically wiped out, and, so far as the Spanish Government is concerned, men go about nearly as they please. The insurgents and their sympathizers will unquestionably take advantage of the revocation to get from the towns and cities what they need, and otherwise strengthen their cause.

The effect on agricultural pursuits will be disappointing, because the great majority of those who would or should take up the work joined the insurgent forces when compelled to leave their homes, and the portion which came within the lines of reconcentration are women, children, old and sickly people, most of whom seem to have little interest in the problem of life. * * * There is no one to take these people back to the fields and utilize their remaining strength. Their houses are destroyed, their fields are overgrown with weeds, they have no seed to plant, and if they had, they can not live sixty or eighty days until the crop matures, which, when grown, would more than likely be taken by one or the other of the contending parties.

Many of those who are attached to their families have them within the insurgent lines.

  * * * * * * *

Finally, I give it as my opinion, an opinion that I am sure is not biased in favor of Cuba, that Spain will be compelled to prosecute a far more vigorous war than has yet been done if she conquers peace in Cuba. I think I speak advisedly when I say that in this end of the island at least there are many thousand square miles where the foot of the Spanish soldier has never trod. Within this zone the insurgents have their families, carol their horses and cattle and raise their crops. They reach the outside world by methods of their own.

Why Spain with a large body of as obedient and brave soldiers as ever shouldered a gun has not penetrated these grounds and scattered to the four winds the comparatively small body of men who are there, is a question I will not attempt to answer.

As I write a man is dying on the street in front of my door, the third in a comparatively short time.

Very respectfully,   PULASKI F. HYATT,
United States Consul.

Mr. Hyatt to Mr. Day.

No. 415.]   CONSULATE OF THE UNITED STATES,
Santiago de Cuba, December 21, 1897.

SIR: I respectfully report that sickness and the death rate on this island is appalling. Statistics make a grievous showing, but come far short of the truth.

The principal disease is known by various names. Calentura, baludol fever, la grippe, etc., is thought by physicians to be brought on by insufficient food. I know some that are attacked that have plenty. These, however, usually make a good recovery, while the others die or make very slow recovery.

The disease is endemic rather than of a zymotic or contageous character. From 30 to 40 per cent of the people are afflicted with it at the present time.

Yellow fever continues in all parts of the island, and smallpox in some places, but are insignificant as compared with the prevailing disease. Out of a total of 16,000 soldiers recently sent to Manzanillo, nearly 5,000 are in hospitals or quartered on the people. I have not learned whether it has attacked the insurgents or not; presumably yes, for Cubans elsewhere are not exempt, as in yellow fever.

An extremely strong effort is being made to increase the strength of the autonomist party. The governor sends for men of supposed influence and asks them to join the party and work to make it successful. He argues that it is a patriotic duty in which all good citizens should aid.

*   *   *   *   *   *   *

As yet planters are all at sea as to whether they will grind cane or not. It is no secret that they will have to make terms with the insurgents if they do, and I understand that an agreement by which 50 cents per bag, or about 15 cents per 100, will be paid for Cuban hands off. Planters say this will leave them no profit, but leave their plantations in better order for future operations.

The three Rivery brothers, American citizens and owners of coffee, cocoa, and orange groves, are about to return to their places. They are absolutely penniless, and say they would have surely starved but for the food issued from this consulate. I shall continue to supply them with food, and issue a month's rations of such food as rice, beans, codfish, crackers, etc., as their homes are over 30 miles away. I have made myself, personally (not my Government), responsible for the transportation of themselves, their families, and goods, as it seemed desirable to get them on their estates as soon as possible.

Dr. Henry S. Caminero, United States sanitary inspector, has just informed me that there are in this city over 12,000 persons sick in bed, not counting those in military hospitals. This is at least 35 per cent of the present population. Quinine, the only remedy of avail, is sold ten times higher than in the States.

Steamers coming to this port mostly give out soup once a day to the waiting throngs.

Fresh meat in our markets sells from 50 cents to $1 a pound.

* * * * * * *

Very respectfully,

PULASKI F. HYATT,
United States Consul.

Mr. Hyatt to Mr. Day.

No. 418.] CONSULATE OF THE UNITED STATES,
Santiago de Cuba, January 1, 1898.

SIR: I have the honor to say that, from a military standpoint, there is nothing new worthy of report, except the mobilization of the Spanish forces to the number of 18,000 in and near Manzanillo, 6,000 of which are in hospital.

Autonomy has been pushed with great vigor, almost or quite to the point of forcing men to join the party, when they could not be hired by a minor office.

When here, a few days since General Pando sent for a Mr. Lora and said: "You have two active and influential brothers in the rebel army. You must go at once to these brothers and say, Come in and join the autonomist party and they will be provided for by me."

Mr. Lora replied: "General, I ran away from my home to escape joining the insurgents; my brothers chose to join them. I will obey your command if you desire to sacrifice my life. My brothers would order me shot on the spot if I approached them with your proposition." General Pando withdrew his command.

Enrique Capeiles, who was governor of this province some four years ago, returned to the same position about a month since. He is highly respected by all classes, and has worked with great energy to build up the autonomist party. He resigned to-day and took a solemn oath that he would never again set foot on Cuban soil. He declared himself both discouraged and disgusted.

The problem of sugar making in this province is most discouraging. Climatic fevers still hold about one-third of the people in bed. The death rate for the week in this city is 109. I deem myself fortunate in being a physician when called upon to fight life's battles amid such surroundings.

Very respectfully, PULASKI F. HYATT,
United States Consul.

Mr. Hyatt to Mr. Day.

No. 420.] CONSULATE OF THE UNITED STATES,
Santiago de Cuba, January 8, 1898.

SIR: I have the honor very respectfully to say that in my opinion the most important question of the Cuban problem to-day is, "Will the people of Cuba accept autonomy as a basis of settlement?"

I have taken great pains to inform myself on this question and to eliminate as far as possible the bias which comes with the sources of my information.

That the Spanish Government has made a most energetic and thorough campaign to make autonomy successful there is no room for doubt. Personal appeals of provincial governors and other important officers have been made earnestly and often to the same individuals. * * * Wholesale removals of Spanish officers from civil positions are made by sweeping orders, with instructions to fill their places with Cuban autonomists. About a week since there came an order dismissing every employee of the custom-house in this city, to take effect as soon as proper autonomists could be found to fill their places.

As yet only two have been named, the collector and first deputy. Against these a strong remonstrance was at once sent in, so the entire old corps are still in place.

The newly appointed provincial governor, Lopez Chavez, has been here for several days, but as yet has not taken charge of the office.

In many cases where Cubans are anticipating the acceptance of an office they have sent to the field to ask permission from insurgent officers.

It will be seen that Cubans are moving very slow in accepting autonomy.

* * * * * * *

It is given out that sometime in the month of February there will be an election held for the purpose of electing sixty members of the Cuban assembly and eighteen members of the council of administration, while seventeen additional ones are to be appointed by the Governor-General. The lines are supposed to be drawn for or against autonomy. Cuban leaders declare they will neither make nominations nor go near the polls; so, if they adhere to their purpose, it will be no test of strength, and no recognition of the result will be taken by the men in the field.

* * * * * * *

Numerous dead bodies at the cemetery are carried over from day to day because the sexton is unable to bury them with his present corps of assistants as fast as they come.

Very respectfully,

PULASKI F. HYATT,
United States Consul.

Mr. Hyatt to Mr. Day.

No. 424.]
CONSULATE OF THE UNITED STATES,
Santiago de Cuba, January 12, 1898.

SIR: I deem it a duty to lay before the honorable Department of State the situation here as affecting American interests, and to inclose herewith an order issued by command of Gen. Maximo Gomez, and a translation of the same, forbidding the grinding of the sugar crop for the years 1897 and 1898.

In this part of Cuba, so far as I can learn, all idea of making a sugar crop is entirely abandoned.

I regret to say that the stoppage of industries, from present appearances, will not halt at the sugar crop, but coffee and other agricultural crops fall under the same ban.

I had hoped that after the reconcentration order was revoked, through the energetic action of the present administration, we would find no trouble in reinstating American industries; but it appears that all of the benefits that should have accrued to our citizens are thwarted by the action of the insurgents, who refuse to allow them to return to their sugar, coffee, and other estates. The Pompo Manganese mines, owned by Americans, would at the present time be a very profitable investment if allowed to operate, are also being held up by the same power.

The three Revery brothers, who I informed you recently I was about to assist in returning to their coffee and fruit estates, got there only to find they could not go to work until permission was obtained from the insurgent commander, which permission seems doubtful, I myself, as I understand my duty, being inhibited from rendering them any assistance at this point.

These, with several sugar estates within my consular district, are held up and becoming more worthless than before.

* * * * * * *

It is beyond the power of my pen to describe the situation in eastern Cuba. Squalidity, starvation, sickness, and death meets one in all places. Beggars throng our doors and stop us on the streets. The dead in large numbers remain over from day to day in the cemeteries unburied.

* * * * * * *

Very respectfully,
PULASKI F. HYATT,
United States Consul.

[Inclosure in No. 421.]

There is a seal that reads: Republic of Cuba, War No. 43, book 3, folio 150.

The council of the Government in session on the 29th day of last month adopted the following resolution:

Considering that the working of the sugar estates favor the plans of our enemies, as shown by the marked interest in their last winter campaign, thus injuring the steady headway of the revolution.

It has been ordered by our Government as a general political measure of war, which to-day is more than ever imposed upon us, and in accordance with article 22, paragraph 6, of the constitution to absolutely prohibit the realization of the sugar crop of 1897-98, that this be communicated to the general-in-chief, with the object that he will dictate the opportune orders for the exact compliance of this resolution, and that it should be published for general knowledge, making known that violators will suffer the punishment prescribed by our laws.

What I transcribe to you for your knowledge and exact compliance.

I am, with high consideration,
Country and liberty,
Palmarito, December 2, 1897.

JOSE B. ALEMAN, *Secretary of War.*

To Gen. CALIXTO GARCIA.

I hereby certify that the above resolution authorized by the secretary of war, José B. Aleman, and directed to Gen. Calixto Garcia, is an exact copy of original on file in the archives of the chief of the military department of Orient.

Bairo, December 28, 1897.

Lieut. Col. EDUARDO SALAZAR, *Auditor.*

Mr. Hyatt to Mr. Day.

No. 424.]
CONSULATE OF THE UNITED STATES,
Santiago de Cuba, January 22, 1897.

SIR: I have the honor to report that Colonel Masso of the insurgent forces, whose home is in this city, has, at a point west of here, given himself up to the Spanish forces, with one hundred and ten officers and men under his command.

Citizens of Santiago say that he did the same thing in the former rebellion.

But the military situation is completely overshadowed in importance by the starving, struggling mass, whose cry is "Bread, or I perish." This consulate is besieged to an extent that blocks the entrance, and greatly retards business. They have heard that the people of the United States are giving funds for their relief, and have not the patience to wait. I could name three Americans here who contribute monthly over three hundred dollars toward feeding the poor, but it is as nothing compared to the people's necessities.

Men, women, and children, homeless and almost naked, roam the streets by day, begging of everyone they meet, or door they pass, and sleeping at night anywhere they can find a place to lie down.

If the present death rate is continued, there would not be a soul left in the city at the end of five years.

For the masses it is speedy help or sure death.

Very repectfully,

PULASKI F. HYATT,
United States Consul.

Mr. Hyatt to Mr. Day.

No. 427.] CONSULATE OF THE UNITED STATES,
Santiago de Cuba, January 31, 1898.

SIR: I desire to inform the honorable Department of State that Captain-General Blanco arrived at this port on Friday night, the 28th instant, but remained on shipboard until the next morning.

The consular corps called soon after his arrival. Most of General Blanco's remarks were directed to the French and American consuls.

* * * * * * *

Colonel Marsh, of General Blanco's staff, called upon and dined with me the same evening. He speaks fairly good English, and is a gentleman of rare social qualities. On leaving he said, "I shall be at all times most happy to use whatever influence I may have with General Blanco in securing a favorable resolution of any matters that you may desire to present to him."

I told him I was prepared to take advantage of his offer at once, as there had just arrived at the custom-house in this place a quantity of quinine which the collector of customs said he could not deliver duty free without instructions from Havana. The colonel promised to lay the matter at once before the Captain-General, and the quinine is released, and, as I understand, it is ordered that all future shipments are to be promptly delivered to me, if any shall come.

On Sunday morning the regular passenger train on the Sabanilla and Maroto Railroad, when 5 miles out of Santiago, was blown up by dynamite bombs, exploded by electric wires; two cars were shivered in atoms. Five passengers were killed outright and twenty-two badly wounded, some of whom have since died. It is thought by some that the insurgents believed that Captain-General Blanco was on the train; by others that they merely wanted to notify the general that they were around and attending to business.

I am, etc.,

PULASKI F. HYATT,
United States Consul.

Mr. Hyatt to Mr. Day.

No. 428.]　　　　CONSULATE OF THE UNITED STATES,
　　　　　　　　Santiago de Cuba, February 1, 1898.

SIR: The military conditions here upon the surface are not materially changed, but to one who watches the signs of the times and knows the character of the men who act the drama the situation is not without portent.

The era of good feeling is passing away, while bitter words and cruel acts are again coming to the front. Those engaged in works of mercy are denounced for keeping alive a tribe that ought to be dead. But it can not be said there is no excuse for harsh judgment. The stoppage of all agricultural pursuits and the blowing up of cars containing innocent people can not be justified even under the guise of war. Extremists of both sides seem able to dominate the sentiments of their respective parties, while a deep feeling of personal hatred pervades their breasts.

General Blanco's mild and humane policy meets with but a feeble response from his own followers, while the insurgents laugh at the old man who throws sods and grass instead of stones.

Autonomy is already a dead issue, while buying insurgent leaders thus far is not a marked success, the insurgent generals having already imprisoned several officers suspected of venality.

Colonel Marsh, of General Blanco's staff, said recently—

> Spain fails to comprehend that Cuba has, as it were, two mothers—a political one, which is Spain; a commercial one, which is the United States; and the political mother fails to see that the commercial mother has any rights, while the commercial mother can not shake off her responsibility, for God has made them next-door neighbors.

I do not believe that the Western Continent has ever witnessed death by starvation equal to that which now exists in eastern Cuba.

Very respectfully, etc.,
　　　　　　　　　　　　　　　　PULASKI F. HYATT,
　　　　　　　　　　　　　　　　　United States Consul.

Mr. Hyatt to Mr. Day.

No. 432.]　　　　CONSULATE OF THE UNITED STATES,
　　　　　　　　Santiago de Cuba, February 15, 1898.

SIR: In the matter of distribution of American relief, I have to report that up to the present time nothing but medicines have reached us; but I understand that food is on the way.

As soon as I learned that quinine was coming I at once addressed a polite note to his excellency informing him of the fact and requesting him to suggest through what channels it would be best to make distribution.

The governor answered very politely, but said, as they had their own physicians who were looking after the poor he did not see the necessity, but should the emergency arise would be very glad to avail himself of the generous offer.

Fortunately, a well organized corps of the first ladies of the city were doing the best they could with the means at hand to help the unfortunates, and to nearly every family in this part of Cuba quinine was as acceptable as gold. Twenty of these ladies called on me for quinine and were at once spreading it among the needy sick. I also sent a quantity to the archbishop, and begged him to accept and use it in such a way as in his judgment he thought best.

The physicians of the city quickly joined, and in less than twenty-four hours the quinine was in every part of the city doing its work.

I also shipped portions to Baracoa on the north coast, to Guanatanamo and Manzanillo on the south coast, to the interior towns of Holguin, Canez, San Luis, Dos Caminos, Cristo, Moron, Dos Bocas, San Vicente, Noniato, and Cuabitas, as also to the towns at Daigneri and Juragua, belonging to two large American iron-mining companies.

A fair quantity was sent to the eleemosynary institutions of this city and other places, so that within a week the whole hundred thousand pills were doing duty and just as they were gone another batch arrived.

The governor, seeing the good work being done, sent me a polite note, saying he had appointed two gentlemen to assist me and that he himself was personally at my service. I then appointed two gentlemen, Dr. Arze and Mr. Octaviano Duany, to act in conjunction with the governor's committee.

These gentlemen will under my direction look after the business matters and will take charge of the distribution of food.

The ladies will go from house to house and issue tickets according to their best judgment, and at certain times these orders will be filled under the direction of the gentlemen committee.

With the free use of quinine the death rate of the city fell 20 per cent the first week.

The quinine and other medicines sent have proved to be so potent and certain in their action, that the work of American chemists has received a decided boom and by all parties the action has been pronounced marvelous.

The doctors have heretofore found that in order to break a fever they had to prescribe from 60 to 100 grains of quinine each day. One-fifth of that amount of American quinine does the work better.

Very respectfully,

PULASKI F. HYATT,
United States Consul.

Mr. Hyatt to Mr. Day.

No. 434.]   CONSULATE OF THE UNITED STATES,
Santiago de Cuba, February 16, 1898.

SIR: Wounded Spanish soldiers, about 200 in number, have been brought to the hospital of this city within the last three days. A surgeon who has dressed the wounds of a Spanish captain tells the story this morning as follows:

Our command, about 7,000 in number, had been to Holquin and were returning, when at a point near Aguacate, without any notice or knowledge of the presence of the enemy in force, a galling fire opened on us, and, as we could not tell from where it came or see the enemy to return the fire, we were ordered to drop flat on the ground. From this position we returned the fire as best we could for a time on an unseen enemy, who finally withdrew.

The captain admitted a loss of 300 in killed and wounded on the Spanish side, and says they have no knowledge of the loss inflicted on the insurgents.

Sixteen hundred new troops from Spain arrived at this port last night, among them quite a number of young doctors just graduated.
Very respectfully,
PULASKI F. HYATT,
United States Consul.

Mr. Hyatt to Mr. Day.

No. 437.]   CONSULATE OF THE UNITED STATES,
Santiago de Cuba, February 26, 1898.

SIR: I have the honor to herewith inclose for your information a copy of a letter sent yesterday by me to the New York Central Cuban Relief Committee, showing the results of four days' work in distributing rations to the starving poor.

Rations are issued in a court attached to the consulate, the people being admitted by the police through a carriage driveway.

As I write the street is blocked by the hungry throng for nearly a square above and below the entrance.

I have requested the police to admit the most delicate and feeble subjects first, as many of them are unable to stand very long in such a crowd.

I shall if possible get a photographic view of the scene and forward it to the President through your honorable Department.

I am, etc.,
PULASKI F. HYATT,
United States Consul.

Since writing this dispatch (No. 437) I have been informed that the ladies, relief committee have estimated that in this city alone the number who need help is at least 18,000.

HYATT, *Consul.*

[Inclosure in No. 437.]

UNITED STATES CONSULATE,
Santiago de Cuba, February 25, 1898.

NEW YORK CENTRAL RELIEF COMMITTEE.

GENTLEMEN: I desire to make a brief report of the first four days' work in distributing the 101 cases of evaporated cream, 65 cases condensed milk, 100 bags of rice, 104 cases of codfish, 6 boxes of bacon, 208 bags flour, 43 barrels of beans, pills, drugs, etc., which I received in due time by steamship *Niagara.*

As stated in a previous communication, a committee of 30 of the best ladies of this place divided the city into 15 districts, with two ladies to each district. These issue rations tickets according to the number of needy persons in each house.

These tickets are honored under the direction of a committee of gentlemen and myself, and a liberal week's rations are issued to each.

To prevent imposition we are obliged to refuse all who do not come with tickets from the ladies. The first day, rations were issued to 379; second day, 579; third day, 1,083; fourth day, 1,027; total, 3,068.

Each ration being for seven days, which makes a total of 21,482 for one day.

As near as I can judge only about one-half of the people who need help have yet received their first rations, and the codfish and beans will give out before we get around the first time.

Have given moderate quantities to the eleemosynary institutions of the city, and sent some to the mining and other towns near by.

We are trying to make both food and medicine do the most good possible.

It takes six or eight policemen to keep the crowds in order.

I am obliged to spend some money for labor, cartage, transportation, cable incidentals, etc.

44　CUBAN CORRESPONDENCE.

There are numerous people badly ruptured and in a distressed condition. I am skilled in handling trusses, but I hardly think it advisable to send trusses, as each case needs a stock to select from.

I would not advise sending any more medicine except quinine for the present. Everything sent has been of a superior quality. The Highland brand of condensed cream and flour are specially fine.

The medicines have had almost miraculous effects. Should you make further shipments, keep beans, rice, and codfish in the foreground, but everything comes in play.

Smallpox has again broken out, and I have requested Surgeon-General Wyman to send to you for me a quantity of vaccine virus. Should it come to hand I will thank you to furnish me with a moderate quantity.

I am, gentlemen, with highest consideration, your most obedient servant,

PULASKI F. HYATT,
United States Consul.

Mr. Hyatt to Mr. Day.

No. 439.]　　　CONSULATE OF THE UNITED STATES,
Santiago de Cuba, March 24, 1898.

SIR:

*　　*　　*　　*　　*　　*　　*

Three sugar estates owned or managed by the house of Brooks & Co. are making sugar on a small scale, but have little faith in their ability to go ahead. These plantations are located near Guantanamo.

Property holders, without distinction of nationality, and with few exceptions, strongly desire annexation, having but little hope of a stable government under either of the contending forces, and they view with regret the indifference, nay, repugnance, of the American people to such a union, and still hope that a combination of circumstances will yet bring it about; but such a move would not be popular among the masses.

On Sunday last an election was held in this city to elect officers to hold an election on the 27th instant. No one seemed to know anything about it until it was over, and the autonomists won the election. A member of that party told me that "we met quietly and done our voting." There is no evidence that the people in general intend to take any part in the coming election. Circulars are now out urging the people to turn out and sustain the government, to the end that peace and prosperity may speedily come.

Very respectfully,

PULASKI F. HYATT,
United States Consul.

Mr. Jora to Mr. Day.

No. 261.]　　　CONSULATE OF THE UNITED STATES,
Sagua la Grande, November 11, 1897.

SIR: It may not be improper that I give the Department my impressions of the status of affairs here concerning the new policy promised by Spain to this island.

By the attitude openly demonstrated against autonomy from the two only existing parties that have to decide its results, the Cuban separatists, including the armed men in the field and their supporters in the towns, and the Spanish conservatives, with followers in Cuba and Spain, the former refusing anything but independence, the latter encouraging its members to strongly protest, not solely against autonomy, but even "reforms," which they have rebuked as contrary to their constitution, I can not help to foresee that far from improving the actual condition of things it will make it more and more critical.

I have left aside without consideration a new factor on the political arena, "annexation," not being able to calculate its magnitude on account of the legal prohibition of that doctrine resulting in the secret endeavors of the adherents, but it is well seen that it is growing stronger every day, principally among the Spaniards. The autonomist part to-day in this district does not exist. In very rare exceptions one partisan may be found loyal to that platform; more so now, in view of Captain-General Weyler's work. It may be said that it is only nominal.

The Reformists have divided themselves so much that its members are to be found in any of the other parties. They are ready to adopt the flag of the more favorable side, turning out thus a very weak association. Spain has to depend on these two last nominal and feeble corporations for the implantation of its new course of action. Taking all these facts into appreciation, it is hard to see in what way is Spain going to establish this new system. It will always be a parasite without stable foundation, without basis, singly maintained by a very infirm, insignificant auxiliary.

In the meantime the reconcentrados, the majority innocent beings, who have had, and even now have no notion of the cause of this revolution, who had no more aspiration than to till their little farms, continue perishing. It is difficult, it may be said almost impossible, to be able to describe the extension and intensity of such tremendous suffering, of such iniquitous, unjust, and sinful imposition, to annihilate thousands of women and children. If this Godless combination should be accurately represented it would seem an exaggeration induced by stirred fellow-feeling. With sensibility in the heart moving among them, the unceasing crowd of famished beggars, one can scarcely do more than commiserate the undeserved misfortune. To express, to delineate the afflictions, the anguishes witnessed at every step, would require much to write, and no lavish of colors could approach the reality to fiction. No history in the world, ancient or modern, can be compared an instant to this frightful, dreadful suffering. Perhaps civilization has not seen the like of it.

In conclusion, I beg to be permitted to state that, in my humble judgment, the efforts toward the enforcement of reforms or autonomy will prove altogether futile; and, of course, in consequence of this failure the few reconcentrados that have survived will not be allowed to go freely to their devastated farms, prolonging thus this unbearable situation.

I have, etc,

JOHN F. JOVA,
Vice-Consul.

Mr. Barker to Mr. Day.

No. 264.] CONSULATE OF THE UNITED STATES,
Sagua la Grande, November 20, 1897.

SIR: I have the honor to submit the following: While General Blanco has made known his purpose to relieve the concentrated people, by allowing them to go out of the towns, it may not be improper that

I give the Department reasons why this permission will not give the relief claimed by the authorities.

While Article I grants permission to this starving class to return to the country, Article III abrogates this very article in exacting that to avail themselves of the privilege the places to which they go must be garrisoned. This condition alone will preclude over one-half of these poor unfortunates, for their homes are in ruin, and the sugar estates able to maintain a guard can care for but a small percentage of the whole.

* * * * * * *

The guerrillas have already started their merciless warfare, having within the past week killed two "presentados" who had in good faith surrendered and gone to work on the American-owned estate "Victoria," repeating the act upon three insurgents who had surrendered to the local guerrillas of Sagua.

I will not question the good intention of those now in power; yet it is a self-evident fact that the authorities are utterly helpless to extend any relief to those who have thus far survived the pangs of hunger. Without instant pecuniary assistance * * * all efforts to relieve the starving populace must fall stillborn. So far as relates to this section of the island, the claim made by the Captain-General through a published letter to the Spanish minister in Washington that "extensive zones of cultivation have been organized, daily rations are provided by the State, work is furnished," etc., is not borne out by my observation.

* * * * * * *

As to grinding the present crop, I have interviewed most of the largest planters in this consular district, who stated that unless assured of immunity from the insurgent chief—Gomez—they would not jeopardize their property by attempting to grind.

It is an unquestioned fact that the military are powerless to give this necessary protection.

I am, etc.,   WALTER B. BARKER,
                                           Consul.

Mr. Barker to Mr. Day.

No. 266.]   CONSULATE OF THE UNITED STATES,
                         Sagua la Grande, November 25, 1897.

SIR: With reference to the distress and deaths in this island, I beg to submit the following relative to this—Santa Clara—province.

As has been my custom for the past five months, I have just made the monthly trip of investigation in this consular district, embracing a large part of the territory of the province. Appended is the official mortality list of each of the judicial districts comprising the province known as "Cinco Villas" (five towns) from January 1 to November 15, 1897, inclusive, viz:

Santa Clara	27,900		Sancti Espiritus	5,482
Sagua	16,583		Trinidad	4,916
Cienfuegos	14,263			
Remedios	11,415		Total	80,589

Add to this 25 per cent for the number of which no record has been kept. * * * I deem a conservative estimate would make the grand total 100,736 deaths.

In truth, after talking with both military and judicial officers, I regard this rather under than above the actual deaths for the period stated.

Undoubtedly one-half the concentrated people have died; and to-day Spanish soldiers are companion victims to the surviving noncombatants.

The inclosed slip (inclosure No. 1), showing the number of deaths, official, in the small municipal district of San Juan de la Yeras, will give some idea of the rapid increase from month to month, as will also the clippings (inclosure No. 2), cut from the local papers, show that the authorities no longer conceal these facts, as was done under the retired Captain-General. This appalling death roll is mute, yet convincing, proof of the terrible destruction of life under the main policy pursued in attempting to subjugate the island. The heavens, it would appear, weep for despoiled, distressed Cuba, for during the present month the fall of rain has been almost phenomenal. I have to reiterate, the authorities, however great the desire to do so, are utterly helpless to ameliorate the dire distress that must continue to increase. * * *

Relative to furnishing protection to the mills to grind, how is it possible in view of the fact that the safeguard extended planters in making the previous crop enabled them to grind less than one-third of the usual yield, while the military force available to-day is not half in numbers as at that time.

With me the conviction is firmly rooted that within sixty days 90 per cent of the populace will reach a state of craving hunger, without outside aid, nor do I feel that I am speaking chimerically when I include the rank and file of the Spanish army.

The true status, as viewed at present, will bear out this opinion. The suffering among the troops, as well as the reconcentrados, simply beggars portrayal, while discontent ripens daily.

I am, etc.,

WALTER B. BARKER,
Consul.

[Inclosure 1 in No. 266.]

Number of deaths each month from January 1 to November 15, 1897, in the municipal district of San Juan de las Lleras.

[Reported officially.]

January	17	August	366
February	18	September	377
March	17	October	417
April	55	November—to 15th	275
May	117		
June	265	Total	2,267
July	313		

[Enclosure 2 in No. 266.—Translation.]

VARIOUS NEWS.

During the month of October last 886 deaths occurred in Santa Clara. There were 44 births only.

HORROR.

El Universo, a daily constitutional paper, which is published in Santa Clara, says: In the month of October last 886 persons died at Santa Clara.

This is the natural consequence of one of the many humanitary proceedings of Weyler—the "concentration" without food. And this is said by El Universo, the Union constitutional daily paper, etc., etc. Horror!

Mr. Barker to Mr. Day.

No. 270.] CONSULATE OF THE UNITED STATES,
Sagua la Grande, December 13, 1897.

SIR: Confident of the desire of the Department to keep in touch with affairs under the new régime, I beg to submit the following:

In order either to qualify or confirm my No. 264, of the 20th instant, wherein I stated the claim made by the authorities that the people were cultivating the soil, rations issued daily to the needy, and protection given to the mills so as to grind the present crop was not in accordance with my observations, I have within the past few days visited five of the principal railroad towns in this consular district—viz, Santa Clara, Cruces, Esperanza, Jicotea, and Santo Domingo. The destitution is simply too harrowing to recite and must become intensified each day. The death rate for last month shows an increase of about 25 per cent.

In these towns I got my information from the mayors of each. From them I learned that while an issue of food, running from three to five days, had been made, beginning on the 28th ultimo, consisting of 3 ounces bacon or jerked beef and 6 ounces rice for adults, with half this allowance for children under 14 years, the pittance given was sufficient only for one-fourth to one-tenth of the starving. No further relief has been given up to date. On the contrary, the mayors of Santa Clara, Cruces, and Santo Domingo are authority for stating the Captain-General had ordered that after the 8th instant any issue of food to the "concentrados" be discontinued. I inclose herewith a clipping from a local paper of Santa Clara confirming this. I have also read it in more than one other Spanish journal.

The mayor of Santa Clara stated to me that the Captain-General a week since directed him to call on the commissary of the army for 5,000 rations for relief purposes, which he said was sufficient to feed the suffering people but for one day. This officer's answer was he could not do so, as all Government supplies on hand would be required to feed the army. The mayor stated, also, that in presenting this order to the military commander he was ordered by him under no circumstances to give food to anyone having relatives in the insurrection, which he informed me would exclude 75 per cent of the destitute. I know that in Sagua and other points orders for food have been given on the commissary departments of the army, but invariably refused, as being needed for the soldiers. I reiterate, however sincere be the authorities to provide for the large number of "concentrados" who dare not return to the country, the fact that they are utterly powerless to do so can not be disguised.

All efforts so far to obtain relief by popular subscription have met with signal failure. The Cubans are too poverty-stricken, while the Spaniards, who own the wealth, will contribute nothing.

In my recent trip I found that the Spanish soldiers are not only suffering for necessary food, but I was often appealed to by these pitiable creatures for medicine. One has only to look upon them to be assured of the needs complained of.

In view of the foregoing facts, known to me from personal investigation, I desire to renew the suggestion made to the Department in a previous dispatch, that the dire destitution and distress of * * * the people * * * appeals for immediate assistance to a charitable, Christian people, with which I sincerely hope the Department may not deem ill-advised to acquaint the people of the United States, when such a response will be made as will bring succor to a starving populace.

* * * * * * *

It is proper that I inform the Department that, added to the universal destitution, the guerrillas continue to attack and kill the noncombatants. * * * As stated, the guerrilla chiefs Carreras, Olavarieta, and Lazo are, if possible, more active in their cruel warfare on "pacificos." I am, etc..

WALTER B. BARKER,
Consul.

[Inclosure 1 in No. 270.—Translation.—From La Patria, December 4, 1897, of Santa Clara.]

ENDING OF RATIONS.

An order has been received from His Excellency the Captain-General directing that from the 8th instant the issue of rations to reconcentrados will be discontinued.

[Inclosure 2 in No. 270.—From Diario de la Marina, December 13, 1897.]

News from the insurrection by our special reporters.

[From Manzanillo, December 9.]

General Pando, from what may be gleaned by his first steps in the district, intends to begin an active campaign.

The task that this worthy general undertakes is very hard, as he finds himself in a part of the country where during two years they have done nothing but protect supply trains, giving the enemy time to perfectly organize themselves, a condition they possess, get together ammunition, and establish great plantations, where they want nothing.

Bear in mind that in saying this I do not try to blame the action of various division generals who have worked; enough have they achieved to hold on, without means of any kind and with forces devoured almost entirely by exhaustion and feebleness.

Another of the great obstacles that the general will find opposed is the absence of strategical places for provisioning the troops, because Yara, Zazzal, Cuentas, Claras, and others equally necessary now were destroyed.

Be it known that the destruction of these towns was effected by order of General Weyler.

[Translation.]

SANTIAGO DE CUBA, *December 8.*

Grinding.—The sugar estates Union and Santa Clara, the only ones that can work this crop, do not show yet any indications that they shall prepare for work. Both are deprived of oxen, it being very difficult to acquire them now in this neighborhood.

Meat.—Yesterday this eatable was selling at 50 cents silver per pound—a short one.

AURELIO.

Mr. Barker to Mr. Day.

No. 271.] CONSULATE OF THE UNITED STATES,
Sagua la Grande, December 15, 1897.

SIR: Thinking it may interest the Department, I have the honor to transmit herewith clippings from a leading Spanish journal published in Havana, * * * calling attention to the inability of the mills to grind in the Province of Santiago de Cuba, which is one of the obstacles to grinding in this (Santa Clara) province, were the planters able to pay tribute required by the insurgents.

The grinding season being at hand without preparations having been made dissipates all hope of a beginning.

H. Doc. 406——4

Not to grind the present crop, small as it must be, will bring distress far greater than can be imagined.

I am, etc.,
WALTER B. BARKER,
Consul.

[Confidential.]

Mr. Barker to Mr. Day.

CONSULATE OF THE UNITED STATES,
Sagua la Grande, December 28, 1897.

SIR: I ask, very respectfully, to submit the following for your consideration:

Since the advent of the new government in this island I have endeavored to keep the Department informed of its workings in this consular district, and province as well.

Thus far every material fact reported has been verified. The suffering and destitution among the concentrados * * * is fearful, and must continue to grow worse.

How could the situation be otherwise, since the island is producing absolutely nothing, save some growing cane, and at the same time completely exhausted of all food. Relief alone can be obtained from the outer world in the way of charitable contributions.

This—Santa Clara—province is capable this season of producing, perhaps, two-thirds of whatever cane might be made in the entire island.

To grind this cane without interruption would be the means of saving the lives of thousands who, without this or outside aid within the next thirty to fifty days, must die of actual hunger. Over a month since the planters were officially advised of Spain's inability to provide protection in order to operate their mills. This leaves the sugar growers entirely in the hands of the Cubans in revolt, as to whether they will be allowed to grind without hindrance or fear of total destruction of their property. I know that strict orders have been given to subordinate commanders under no circumstances must mills be permitted to grind, under penalty of violation of the order destruction of property.

* * * * * * *

Without contributions of food and medicine from the outer world, and at once, a sacrifice of lives will ensue, the responsibility for which no Christian people can face.

I am, etc.,
WALTER B. BARKER,
Consul.

Mr. Barker to Mr. Day.

No. 273.]
CONSULATE OF THE UNITED STATES,
Sagua la Grande, January 8, 1898.

SIR: I have the honor to transmit herewith, for conformation, copy of my telegram of even date sent the Department through our honorable consul-general at Havana, giving number of paupers in this consular district and province.

Prompt relief in the way of medicines as well as food will save many lives of this unfortunate class. While clothing, as stated, is needful, food and medicines are essential to save life.

Voluntary letters just received from the mayors of four of the principal towns of this immediate zone show not only the necessity for instant succor, but evince an earnest desire on the part of these recently installed officials to render aid in distributing whatever relief the charitable people of the United States may send this suffering people, not forgetting, as I shall not, the many Spanish soldiers whose every appearance is indicative of destitution.

This consular district—due to the fact that nearly thirty towns are embraced in it—will require more or less expenditure of money in lieu of food; yet I am assured of gratuitous transportation for supplies by the Sagua Railroad.

Within a few days I hope to have an official list from the mayors of the number of destitute in their respective municipal districts to forward to the Department.

I am, etc.,
WALTER B. BARKER,
Consul.

[Inclosure 1 in No. 273.—Telegram.]

Mr. Barker to Mr. Day.

SAGUA, *December 8, 1897.*

States that food, medicine, and clothing are required by more than 50,000 persons in his consular district, and that a reliable estimate of the number of starving in the Sagua province is 100,000. Advises the immediate need of relief by supplies through Consul-General Lee at Havana, or directly by the Munson Line. Says that some money will be needed, and that municipal authorities will aid in distributing supplies sent.

BARKER, *Consul.*

[Inclosure 2 in No. 273.]

Mr. Barker to Mr. Lee.

SAGUA, *December 8, 1897.*

DEAR SIR: I hand you herewith a telegram which I beg you will send from your office—by cable—in cipher if you deem best.

I need not tell you that the situation demands immediate action and relief.

I do not transmit this message for the reason I have no cipher "code." A copy of this telegram, with reasons for sending you to be transmitted, will follow in a dispatch to the Department.

Yours, truly,
WALTER B. BARKER,
Consul.

NOTE.—Should the Department not regard it ill-advised, and will telegraph me authority to so act, I can, by wiring message to personal friends in New Orleans, Mobile, Memphis, Chattanooga, Atlanta, and Charleston, obtain needed contributions much more promptly.

BARKER, *Consul.*

Mr. Barker to Judge Day.

No. 278.]
CONSULATE OF THE UNITED STATES,
Sagua la Grande, January 15, 1898.

SIR: I beg to submit the following: In this consular district a reign of terror and anarchy prevail which the authorities, be they so disposed, are utterly powerless to control or in any measure subdue.

Aside from the suffering and desperation caused by the unparalleled destitution, I regard the situation as rapidly assuming a critical stage;

and to add that, as stated repeatedly heretofore, in no way have the authorities departed, in fact, from the policy pursued by the late (but not lamented) General Weyler. Spanish troops as well as the guerrillas, under the cruel chiefs Carreras, Olavarrieta, and Lazo, continue to despoil the country and drench it with the blood of noncombatants. Although the "bando" of the Captain-General provides that laborers may return to estates having a garrison, last week a number belonging on the "Sta Ana," located within a league of Sagua, and owned by Mr. George Thorndike, of Newport, R. I., were driven off after returning, and refused permit as a protection by the military commander, Mayor Lomo, one of the trusted officers under the Weyler régime.

I am, etc.,
WALTER B. BARKER.

Mr. Barker to Judge Day.

[Confidential.]

CONSULATE OF THE UNITED STATES,
Sagua la Grande, January 10, 1898.

SIR: Pardon the presumption, if presumption it be, in me in offering the following suggestions for the consideration of the Department:

When Spain will admit defeat no mortal, in my humble judgment, dare predict. That her plan of settlement—autonomy—is a failure, and with this failure passes from under her dominion the island, is not to be questioned.

Pending this admission on her part, thousands of human beings, guiltless of bringing on or having any part in the insurrection, are dying for want of sustenance. This condition must continue to increase.

The United States in taking action relative to Cuba—which seems inevitable—desires to avoid a clash with Spain. Then let Congress alter our citizenship laws by amending the statute relative to the declaration required of persons becoming citizens by naturalization so that the subject or citizens of any government at present residing in Cuba may go before any United States consul in that island and make declaration of intention of becoming a citizen of the United States, which shall entitle them to recognition as citizens until the expiration of two years, when they shall be required to reside in the United States until five years shall have elapsed before being granted naturalization papers.

With such a privilege, I am confident 90 per cent of the resident Spaniards—the hitherto dominant party and taxpayers—will avail themselves of this opportunity (as they would have it) of rebuking the mother country for attempting to foist upon them any changes in the existing laws of the island. Such a step would cause the home subjects as well as the Government to acquiesce, without disturbance, in the loss of the island. To this, if none other, there may be constitutional objections.

Again, assuming that Spain may now accept the "good offices" of the United States with a view to negotiating a peace with her rebellious subjects, let an armistice for sixty days be suggested, in which time terms of settlement to be discussed between the authorities and the insurgents, the United States being the umpire.

Pending negotiations, all Spanish troops to be quartered and held in the larger fortified coast towns, in order that the "concentrados" may return to the country to arrange to subsist themselves; for, be it understood, that the proposed relief to be sent from the United States, as well as Government aid now being given our citizens, must be continued or leave the people to starve, so long as there is an armed Spanish soldier in the country, since these people, for fear of being murdered, dare not go to their country homes.

I have the honor, etc.,

WALTER B. BARKER,
Consul.

Mr. Barker to Mr. Day.

No. 284.] CONSULATE OF THE UNITED STATES,
Sagua la Grande, January 27, 1898.

SIR: I beg to inform the Department that smallpox, referred to in my No. 279 of the 18th instant, has increased to an alarming extent.

The number of cases and mortality among the "reconcentrados" is unprecedented throughout this consular district.

I am, etc..

WALTER B. BARKER,
Consul.

Mr. Barker to Mr. Day.

No. 286.] CONSULATE OF THE UNITED STATES,
Sagua la Grande, January 31, 1898.

SIR: Relative to citizens of the United States residing in this consular district, I have the honor to say to the Department, after three months, the new administration's progress and repudiation concerning the abuses in vogue under the former régime reveal the following facts:

Of those herded in the garrisoned towns, none have been allowed to return to their landed estates. Some few who did venture to go to their farms under a pledge of protection from the military commander of the province—to whom I will not impute bad faith—were driven off by guerrillas. * * * At my suggestion several families returned to the American-owned "Central Santa Anna," the owner having been forced to abandon the property in order to prevent further spoliation of the mill machinery. Although a Government guard is stationed on the place, they (former tenants) were ordered to leave.

Application was made to the military commander * * * for authority to return unmolested, which was refused.

Over two months since, two of our citizens notified me they had discovered in possession of the local guerrillas ten or twelve head of their horses, seized by said guerrillas. I addressed the military commander of Sagua, * * * asking, upon proof of ownership, their stock to be restored. Nothing has been done; while these American citizens—both in affluence at the breaking out of the rebellion—are to-day dependent on charity.

One sugar mill is running, not without interruption, with chances of making one-fourth of a crop. Another—just started up—was attacked yesterday by a band of insurgents, killing 14 and wounding 5 of the guerrillas paid by the estate to protect the operatives. Seven laborers were killed, the insurgents leaving two of their dead.

An adjoining estate, the property of the British consul, was also attacked, the growing cane burned. This precludes further attempts to grind, as men can not be induced to work while the insurgents roam at will over the country.

I am, etc.,
WALTER B. BARKER,
Consul.

Mr. Barker to Mr. Day.

No. 288.]
CONSULATE OF THE UNITED STATES,
Sagua la Grande, February 17, 1898.

SIR: I beg to submit the following:

It is proper that I inform the Department that the ravage of smallpox has reached a point where the physicians, few in number, without proper means of treating, as well as no nurses, can not cope with it. I have cabled our dispatch agent in New York for an additional supply of virus.

I was informed by the mayor of this city only yesterday that he was just in receipt of a communication from the government of the province stating no funds to feed the starving were obtainable. In reply to my query why he did not send a number of them to the country, he stated that the military commander refused to grant this permission.

I am, etc.,
WALTER B. BARKER,
Consul.

Mr. Barker to Mr. Day.

No. 294.]
CONSULATE OF THE UNITED STATES.
Sagua la Grande, March 12, 1898.

SIR: With reference to the distribution to and requirement for the concentrados in my consular district, I beg to submit the following for the information of the Department:

From the 15th of last month, through cash donations made to this consulate, direct, through personal appeal, I cared for 1,200 persons. By the 1st instant these contributions increased so as to enable the committee to increase the relief list to 2,000. This has been maintained until now; but as the *Fern*, with 35 tons, should arrive to-morrow, the Sagua relief can be continued.

About a week since I received the first shipment of supplies, about twenty tons being sent from Havana under direction of the Red Cross branch in that city. All this I distributed among ten of the twenty-two towns I had managed to investigate, using none for Sagua; there being five others not yet looked into out of the twenty-seven cities and towns in my zone. I believe that with the assistance of a very able local committee, that I have this relief reduced to a kind of system so as to avoid as little abuse as possible, and at the same time care for the most deserving.

For instance, about sixty days ago, the mayors of these towns furnished, by request, this office with the number they claimed as actually destitute in their several municipal districts, which footed up over 50,000 persons. Estimating a decrease from death of 10,000, would leave, say 40,000.

From the investigation so far made, I estimate if provision can be made to care for 25,000, whatever may be left will manage to survive. Upon this estimate I beg to say that to keep this number alive will require 80 tons per month.

With the supplies reported in transit we can carry them through until the 12th of the coming month (April).

While, as stated in a very recent dispatch to the Department, the military have thrown every conceivable obstacle in the way of carrying out this humane work, I have, when convinced of their sincerity, acted in conjunction with the civil authorities.

Of the 5,000 utterly destitute in this city, the mayor, by popular subscription, has made an effort to issue a scant ration of rice and beans to about one-third of this number. Yesterday he called to say that he had a telegram from the acting Spanish minister in Washington, suggesting that he offer to aid me in the distribution of the supplies being sent from the United States; that he had no funds with which to do anything.

Being a good active man, I gladly accepted the offer of his services.

It is with pleasure that I say to the Department that Senor Leonardo Chia, "administrador" of the Sagua, as also the "administradores" of the Santa Clara and Cienfuegos railroads, have not only transported free the supplies for the reconcentrados, but have used extra effort to have them reach destination in due time.

I am, etc., WALTER B. BARKER,
Consul.

Mr. Barker to Mr. Day.

No. 295.] CONSULATE OF THE UNITED STATES,
Sagua la Grande, March 14, 1898.

SIR: The inclosed letter from Mr. Valle,* of Sancti Espiritus, whom I have every reason to believe will not misrepresent the case, together with the fact that in other places I find I have underestimated the number in my jurisdiction in need of relief. It is therefore that I beg to increase the amount required, as stated in my No. 294, of the 12th instant, from 80 to 100 tons per month.

I am, etc., WALTER B. BARKER,
Consul.

[Telegram.]

Mr. Barker to Mr. Day.

SAGUA LA GRANDE, *March 24, 1898.*

DAY, *Washington:*

Closer investigation disclose larger number destitute than estimates sent. Fifty tons needful now. Distress far greater than my reports show.

BARKER, *Consul.*

---

* Letter referred to implores medicines and provisions.

Mr. Barker to Mr. Day.

No. 297.]   CONSULATE OF THE UNITED STATES,
     Sagua La Grande, March 21, 1898. (Received March 30.)

SIR: I have the honor to say that since forwarding my No. 294 of the 12th instant, wherein I gave the Department approximately the amount of food required for my zone per month, I find many outlying—interior—villages, of which I had no account, neglected and in great want. To this very class, located in the interior towns, I have given special attention, but it has been impossible to care for all immediately. For instance, the relief committee to whom supplies were sent in Santa Clara, seat of government of the province, inform me to-day that in a small town near there are 300 persons in pressing need. To-day I wired Mr. Louis Klopsch, of the Christian Herald and Central Cuban Relief Committee, who is now in Havana, that 20 tons additional required till 1st proximo, and to know if he could supply this. As yet no reply has been received. A very large proportion of these poor creatures being actually ill, other medicine than quinine is required, as also medicinal wines and nourishing food for them.

I beg to inclose herewith a list of towns to which I have and am sending supplies. There are perhaps six to eight more requiring relief.

In this, Sagua la Grande, the number on the relief list exceeds 4,000. The authorities have given up, turning over to my committee their "kitchen," which is being run by them, as is also the "dispensary" for sick children.

The committee inform me since beginning the relief the death rate has fallen from 25 to 30 as low as 4 to 7 per day.

*   *   *   *   *   *   *

I am, sir, your obedient servant,
WALTER B. BARKER,
Consul.

[Inclosure No. 297.]

List of cities and towns being supplied from the consul at Sagua la Grande.

Sagua la Grande.	Sitiecito.	Santo.
Santa Clara.	Rodrigo.	Camajuani.
Santi Spiritus.	Rancho Veloz.	Caibarien.
San Juan de los Remedios.	Carahatas.	Yagnajay.
Esperanza.	Vueltas.	Seibabo.
Cruces.	Vega Alta.	Quemado de Guines.
Santo Domingo.	Vega de Palma.	Caguaguas.
Encrucijada.	Mata.	Ysabela.
Calabazar.	Quinta.	Victoria.
Cifuentes.	Viana.	San Diego del Valle.
Sitio Grande.	Jicotea.	Lajas.

Mr. Barker to Mr. Day.

No. 299.]   CONSULATE OF UNITED STATES,
     Sagua la Grande, March 21, 1898.

SIR: I visited seat of government of this province, Santa Clara, where I learned, not alone from trustworthy persons sent out by me for the purpose, but also the civil governor, that the number of persons in actual want exceeds any estimate I have sent the Department. The distress is simply heartrending. Whole families without clothing to hide nakedness, sleeping on the bare ground, without bedding of any kind, without food, save to such as we have been able to reach with provisions sent by our noble people; and the most distressing feature is that fully 50 per cent are ill, without medical attention or medicine. If $5,000 could be telegraphed to our honorable consul-general at Havana, blankets, cots, and medicine could be purchased here in the several towns adjacent, and save thousands who must die if to await their being sent from the United States. I have found the civil governor willing to lend every aid in his power; but he admits he can do nothing but assist with his civil officers in expediting relief sent by the United States. The military obstruct in every way possible.

* * * The Department will bear in mind the towns I am trying to reach with relief will number over forty.

I am, etc., WALTER B. BARKER,
Consul.

[Gazette of Madrid, Friday, November 26, 1897.]

OFFICIAL.—PRESIDENCY OF THE COUNCIL OF MINISTERS.

STATEMENT.

MADAM: At the time when an autonomic constitution is given to the islands of Cuba and Porto Rico, which intrusts to their own initiative the management and government of their local interests, it is of paramount importance to strengthen constitutional unity, as the staunchest basis on which the integrity of our territory rests.

This aim of all the liberal parties, recognized in principle by the decree of April 2, 1881, has, however, failed of accomplishment in the form to which the people of the Antilles are entitled. They frequently complain of and deplore irritating inequalities which are of themselves sufficient to hamper, if not totally to preclude, the enjoyment of constitutional liberty. Indeed, these liberties, as they are disclosed in the fundamental code, consist of declarations of rights and guarantees that are subsequently sanctioned and developed in a series of organic laws, complements of the constitution, as provided in its fourteenth article, which devolves on special laws "the rules which must secure to the Spaniards reciprocal respect for the rights herein granted, and at the same time determine the civil responsibility and the penalty to which officers of all classes who infringe the rights set forth in Title I must be held liable.

It follows that if, through arbitrary provisions for which no remedy exists, through penalties imposed in the orders of governors-general, or through the omissions of laws of procedure, the citizen may be restrained, molested, or even deported to distant parts of the territory, he finds it impossible to exercise his right to speak, think, and write, or to enjoy freedom of teaching and religious toleration, or to avail himself of the right of meeting and associating.

And yet the whole foundation of modern law rests on the regular and orderly exercise of these rights; therefore, wherever it is limited equality before the law ceases and with it constitutional unity. Then arise these perverted feelings which are carried to the extent of attacking the integrity of the territory. The geographical bond with all its attractions and allurements can not cause that other aspiration to be forgotten, which, while it grows out of the same human instinct, is deeper and more essential.

It is therefore good policy, at all events it is an act of strict justice, to do all that is in the power of the Government, to the end that the Constitution be at once extended in its entirety to the territory of the Antilles, that every vestige of inequality may be removed, and that our legislation be thoroughly revised, so that there can be no Spaniard who, through confusion or error, may lack the protection of the law.

This is certainly the intent of article 89 of the constitution. The provision by which it leaves to the discretion of the governments the time and manner in which the laws are to be applied to the islands of Cuba and Puerto Rico does more than grant the authority; it imposes on the Government the duty to publish this decree at the very time when it submits to your majesty the other measure which is about to give to our brethren in the Antilles—the right to govern themselves. The full value of that measure would not be appreciated if suspicion and distrust, closely followed by arbitrariness, should prevail in the regions of the Central Power.

Inasmuch as we, in the peninsula, have come to the belief that all executive functions can be discharged within the constitution of the State and under the laws enacted for its execution; inasmuch as instances of resort to force, against which, however, the law of public order is deemed adequate, are not lacking here, we should show ourselves to be illogical, and, consequently, lose the authority requisite for forceful government, if we did not proclaim, as the foremost and most significant part of the transformation effected in our colonial régime, that constitutional unity which is the bond that unites all Spaniards, and under which the free local government of those valued territories will restore confidence in the mother country, and thus will unmistakable evidence be given of the sincerity with which she seeks to render her sovereignty beloved.

Resting on the foregoing reasons, the Government has the honor to submit the appended draft of a decree to your majesty's approval.

At the royal feet of your majesty.

PRAXEDES MATEO SAGASTA.

MADRID, *November 25, 1897.*

ROYAL DECREE.

In accordance with the opinion of my council of ministers and by virtue of the authority conferred on my Government by article 89 of the constitution, in the name of My August Son, King Alfonso XIII, and as Queen Regent of the Kingdom, I hereby decree as follows:

ARTICLE 1. The Spaniards residing in the Antilles shall enjoy, on equal terms with the residents of the peninsula, the rights granted in Title I of the constitution of the Monarchy and the guarantees whereby their exercise is secured by the laws of the Kingdom.

To this end, and conformably to article 89 of the constitution, the laws by which its provisions are supplemented, and especially that of criminal prosecution, that of compulsory expropriation, that of public instruction, that of the press, and of meeting and association, and the code of military justice, shall go into full effect in the islands of Cuba and Puerto Rico, so that article 14 of the constitution may be executed in its entirety.

ART. 2. In time of war the law of public order shall be enforced in the Antilles with the limitation and in the manner prescribed in article 17 of the constitution.

ART. 3. The ministry of the colonies, after bearing the council of state, shall revise the legislation of the Antilles and the proclamations published by the Governors-General since the promulgation of the constitution, and shall thereafter publish the results of such revision, to the end that henceforth there may be neither on the part of the executive, nor on that of the judiciary, any possibility, through error or neglect, either of citing or enforcing provisions that are at variance with the letter or spirit of the constitution of the Spanish Monarchy.

MARIA CRISTINA.

The president of the council of ministers:

PRAXEDES MATEO SAGASTA.

Done at the Palace, November 25, 1897.

STATEMENT.

MADAM: The complement of the decree that places the Spaniards on an equal footing as regards the use and enjoyment of their constitutional rights and the indispensable preparation for the organization of local government in the Antilles is the enforcement in those territories of the law of electoral suffrage that is in force in the Peninsula.

To effect this the Government might have confined itself to the reproduction, pure and simple, of that law; but the difficulty of so doing will be apparent when it is remembered that in order to give the greatest security to the electoral right the Cortes of the Kingdom, proceeding with forethought and in their desire to avoid impairing, through seemingly unimportant reglementary provisions, rights that have much value in public life, sought to include in the law even the last and most minute regulations that govern its execution.

For this purpose there are in it two kinds of provisions—one that comprises the definition of the right and the guarantee of the casting of the vote, than other that establishes the conditions, so to speak, preparatory to those purposes. Hence the necessity of discriminating between these two parts of the law.

The first undoubtedly possesses a character that yields in importance to constitutional provisions only, and therefore it must, like these, protect itself from the changes and modifications to which legislation is frequently exposed.

It merely behooves the Government to say that since we have considered it good and proper for the Peninsula, it is an obligation that can not be evaded, to extend it and apply it to our colonies.

The same is not the case, however, as regards the mode of procedure.

So far as it possesses that character in the exercise of suffrage, in the taking of the census, in the manner of casting the vote, in the preliminaries of the election, in the organization of the colleges, even in the qualifications of the electors, there are such different points of view, according to the traditions, the geography, and the component parts of a people, that it would be more than illogical, nay, would lead to a result diametrically opposed to that which is had in view, to shape the electoral procedure of the Antilles in the peninsular mold, especially when the creation of self-government and of parliamentary organisms that are to be the expression of the will of the people demand that the regulation of what relates to the exercise and security of the electoral right be intrusted to them.

In view of these weighty considerations, the Government has thought that after separating all that refers to the definition and recognition of the right of suffrage from what might be called the constitution of the islands of Cuba and Puerto Rico, in order that, in any case, it may be modified by a law, it ought to intrust all the regulations, which will be many in number and complicated in their development, to the insular Parliament, feeling certain that no one possesses to a greater extent the conditions necessary for success in adapting them to the habits and character of the population.

The flexibility thus acquired by the electoral procedure will undoubtedly enable it to identify itself with the conditions of those inhabitants, and to render the exercise of suffrage practical and fruitful, as no one can have more interest in its success than those who are to be governed by it.

On the basis of these considerations, the Government has the honor to submit to the approval of your majesty the accompanying draft of a decree.

At your majesty's royal feet.

PRAXEDES MATEO SAGASTA.

MADRID, *November 25, 1897.*

ROYAL DECREE.

In accordance with the opinion of my council of ministers, and in virtue of the power conferred upon my Government by article 89 of the constitution of the monarchy, in the name of my august son, King Alfonso XIII, and as Queen Regent of the Kingdom, I decree as follows:

ARTICLE I. The electoral law of June 26, 1890, shall be promulgated and observed in the islands of Cuba and Porto Rico, with the modifications that have been introduced in the text that follows this decree, with a view to its adaptation to the conditions of those territories.

ART. II. The regulations and other necessary provisions for the execution of the present decree, which the Government shall   before the Cortes, shall be prepared by the ministry of the colonies.

MARIA CRISTINA.

The president of the council of ministers:

PRAXEDES MATEO SAGASTA.

Done at the Palace this 25th day of November, 1897.

Adaptation of the Electoral Law of June 26, 1890, to the islands of Cuba and Porto Rico.

TITLE I.—GENERAL PROVISIONS FOR ELECTIONS.

CHAPTER I.—*Of the right to vote.*

ARTICLE 1. All male Spaniards over 25 years of age that shall be in the full enjoyment of their civil rights, and inhabitants of a municipal district in which they shall have resided at least two years, shall be voters in the islands of Cuba and Porto Rico.

Soldiers and sailors serving in the army or navy shall not be allowed to vote while so serving.

The same suspension is ordered as regards those serving under similar circumstances in other armed bodies depending on the State, province, or municipality.

ART. II. The following persons shall not be voters:

(1) Those who by an unappealable sentence have been condemned to perpetual deprivation of political rights and public offices, although they may have been pardoned, unless they have previously obtained personal rehabilitation by means of a law.

(2) Those who, by an unappealable sentence, have been condemned to imprisonment, unless they have obtained rehabilitation at least two years before their enrollment in the census.

(3) Those who, having been condemned to other penalties by an unappealable sentence, shall not furnish evidence that they have served out those penalties.

(4) Bankrupts, not rehabilitated according to law, and who do not furnish documentary evidence that they have met all their obligations.

(5) Debtors to public funds as second tax payers.

(6) Those who are inmates of charitable institutions, or who are administratively authorized, at their request, to ask for public charity.

CHAPTER II.—*Of the electoral census.*

ART. 3. In order to exercise the right of suffrage, it is necessary that the person be inscribed in the electoral census; that is to say, the register containing the names and the paternal and maternal surnames, where they exist, of the Spanish citizens who have a right to vote.

The census is permanent, and shall be amended only by the annual revision.

ART. 4. The taking, revision, custody, and inspection of the census shall be under the charge, in accordance with their respective powers, of the central board established by the law of June 26, 1890, concerning provincial boards and of municipal boards, which shall be styled the electoral census boards.

The provincial boards shall sit in the capitals of each province, and the municipal boards shall sit in each municipality. They shall all be of a permanent character.

The provincial boards shall be presided over by the judges of the superior court (audencia) of such province as may be designated by the president of the superior district court to which that audencia belongs; and the municipal boards (shall be presided over) by the judges of first instance, or, in their absence, by public officers selected for that purpose by the president of the superior court of the province.

The number of the members of the provincial boards shall be fifteen, and the presence of nine members shall be requisite for deliberation or for taking action.

The following persons shall be members of the provincial boards:

(1) The president and the vice-president of the deputation concerned.

(2) The senior ex-president of the same deputation residing in the province.

(3) Four taxpayers chosen by lot from among those paying the first assessment of the land tax, who are residents of the province.

(4) Four taxpayers chosen by lot from among those paying the first assessment of the industrial tax, who are residents of the province.

(5) Four residents of the province, furnishing proof by means of official documents, of their professional or academic character.

The substitutes for the taxpayers shall be eight persons residing in the province and paying the largest assessments of the land tax, and eight persons residing in the province and paying the largest assessments of the industrial tax, and the substitutes of the residents having official titles shall be persons possessing the same qualifications as are required of them. They shall all be chosen by lot.

The choice by lot of the taxpayers, professional men and their substitutes shall be made publicly before the superior court of each province by the presiding judge of that court.

The following persons shall be members of the municipal boards:

(1) The alcalde (mayor) and the syndic of the city council.

(2) The municipal judge and the municipal attorney.

(3) Ex-alcaldes residing in the municipal district.

(4) Four of the chief payers of the land tax, and four of the chief payers of the industrial tax, residing in the municipal district.

(5) Four residents of the municipal district, furnishing proof, by means of official documents, of their professional or academic character.

The taxpayers and professional men shall be chosen by lot by the president of the municipal board, at a public meeting, before the city council, in the manner prescribed for the provincial boards.

The substitutes shall be chosen at the same time and in the same manner.

The municipal boards shall not deliberate nor take any action unless at least twelve members are present.

The clerks of the superior courts shall be the secretaries of the provincial boards, and the clerks of the courts of first instance, or, in their absence, the clerks of the municipal courts, shall be the secretaries of the municipal boards.

The secretaries shall have neither a voice nor a vote, and shall be assisted by the employees of the respective secretariats.

The respective presidents shall convene the members and such substitutes as they may deem necessary for all the sessions the boards may hold. If, in spite of this, a sufficient number are not present, the session shall be held on the following day, after the substitutes residing in the capital have been summoned, in addition to the members present.

CHAPTER III.—*Of voting.*

ART. 5. In every electoral precinct there shall be a board charged with the supervision of the voting, consisting of a president and the supervisors (interventores) appointed by the census board and by the candidates who have a right to nominate them, and who make use of that right.

This census board shall be the provincial board in the case of elections of deputies to the Cortes and of representatives or provincial deputies to the Cortes, and of representatives, and the municipal board when an election of councilmen (concejales) is to be held.

ART. 6. In every summons for a general or partial election a single day shall be designated for the voting, which day shall always be Sunday.

The voting shall take place simultaneously in all the precincts on the day fixed, beginning punctually at 8 o'clock in the morning and continuing uninterruptedly until 4 o'clock in the afternoon, when it shall be declared finally closed, and the counting of the votes shall begin.

ART. 7. The voting shall be secret, by ballot, and shall be conducted in the manner prescribed by the regulations.

ART. 8. There shall in no case be an armed force at the door of the electoral college, nor shall any such force enter it, except in the case of disturbance of the public peace and upon the requisition of the President.

TITLE II.—SPECIAL PROVISIONS FOR THE ELECTIONS.

CHAPTER I.—*Of the election of senators.*

ART. 9. Spaniards possessing the qualifications required by article 22 of the constitution of the monarchy, are eligible to the office of senator, provided they are not included in any of the cases of disability or incompatibility fixed by law.

ART. 10. Elections of senators shall be held in accordance with the provisions of the laws of February 8, 1877, and of January —, 1879.

The senators, after they have been admitted by the senate, represent the nation individually and collectively.

CHAPTER II.—*Of the election of deputies to the Cortes.*

ART. 11. All male Spaniards of the secular order, not less than 25 years of age, in the enjoyment of all civil rights, are eligible to the office of deputy to the Cortes, provided they are not included in any of the cases of disability or incompatibility fixed by law.

ART. 12. The deputies to the Cortes shall be elected directly by the electors of the electoral districts, subject to this law and the regulations; but after they have been elected, and admitted by Congress, they represent the nation individually and collectively.

ART. 13. Those provisions of the electoral law of the peninsula of June 26, 1890, which relate specially to the election of deputies to the Cortes and the discharge of their duties, apply to the deputies to the Cortes from the islands of Cuba and Puerto Rico. Hence, the articles in question are inserted as an appendix to the present law, n the form in which they are to be observed in accordance with this law.

CHAPTER III.—*Of the election of counselors of administration, representatives, provincial deputies, and councilmen.*

ART. 14. Those Spaniards may be counsellors of administration and representatives who possess the qualifications required for those offices by the constitution of the islands of Cuba and Porto Rico.

ART. 15. Spaniards having the qualifications required for deputies to the Cortes, and who are natives of the province, or who have resided four years consecutively in the province, may be provincial deputies.

ART. 16. Those electors may be elected members of ayuntamientos (councilmen) in municipal districts containing not more than 100 inhabitants, who, in addition to having resided at least four years in the municipality, pay a direct tax included in the first two-thirds of the local lists of persons paying a land tax, and an industrial and commercial subsidy, and in municipal districts containing less than 1,000 and more than 400 inhabitants, those paying taxes included in the first four-fifths of the said lists. In municipal districts containing not more than 400 inhabitants all the electors shall be eligible.

All those paying a tax equal to the lowest tax required to be paid in each municipal district in order to be eligible under the preceding paragraph shall likewise be included in the number of eligibles.

Those residents who pay any assessment of tax and furnish proof by means of official documents of their professional or academic character shall likewise be eligible.

Those persons who furnish proof that they are subjected to a rebate (reduction) in the incomes which they derive from general, provincial, or municipal funds shall likewise be eligible, provided the amount of the rebate is included in the qualification (proporcion) previously fixed for eligibles in towns of 1,000 and 400 inhabitants, respectively.

The assessment (tax) shall be calculated by adding together the taxes paid by the taxpayers, in and outside of the town, as a direct tax and for municipal taxes (charges). In calculating the taxes of the electors and the eligibles the following property shall be considered as theirs: In the case of husbands, the property of their wives, so long as the conjugal relationship exists; in the case of fathers, such property of their children as they administer legally; in the case of sons, their own property, the usufruct of which they do not enjoy for any reason.

ART. 17. Those persons who are included in any of the cases of disability or incompatibility established by the respective laws can not be elected to any of the offices mentioned in the three preceding articles.

ART. 18. Those persons designated in article 25 of the electoral law of the peninsula relating to senators shall be electors of counselors of administration. The provisions of chapter 4 of that law shall be applied to the drawing up of the lists of electors and to the election of the counselors of administration in the manner prescribed by the regulations.

ART. 19. In the districts in which one representative, one provincial deputy, or one councilman (concejal) is to be elected no elector can legally give his vote to more than one person; when more than one, up to four, are to be elected, each elector shall have the right to vote for one less than the number of those who are to be elected in his own district; for two less (than the number of those who are to be elected) if more than four are to be elected, and for three less when more than eight are to be elected.

The other provisions relative to electoral procedure shall be such as are enacted in the respective organic laws and in the regulations.

TITLE III.—PENAL SANCTION.

CHAPTER I.—*Of offenses.*

ART. 20. Any forgery of documents relating to the provisions of this law, in any of the ways mentioned in article 310 of the penal code of Cuba and Porto Rico, shall constitute the crime of forgery in electoral matters, which shall be punished with the penalties provided in the said article, or in the following article, according to the status of the persons who are responsible.

Any intentional omission in the documents referred to in the preceding paragraph which may affect the result of the election shall constitute a similar offense, and shall be punished with the same penalties.

ART. 21. The courts shall, nevertheless, lessen the penalties one or two degrees, imposing them upon such person as they may think proper, according to the special circumstances of the case, the scandal or alarm that it has occasioned, and whenever there shall appear to be no connection with other offenses made punishable by the code.

ART. 22. For the purposes of this law, the census and authorized copies thereof, records, lists, certificates, and whatever may emanate from the person who is intrusted by law with the execution thereof, the object of which is to facilitate or insure the exercise of the electoral right or its result, or to guarantee the regularity of the procedure, shall be considered official documents.

ART. 23. The penalties of imprisonment and of a fine of from 500 to 5,000 pesetas, when the general provisions of the penal code do not fix a higher penalty, shall be imposed upon public officers who, by failing to faithfully and strictly fulfill the obligations imposed by this law or by the provisions that may be adopted for its execution, are accessory to any of the following acts or omissions:

(1) To any failure to prepare with accuracy the lists of electors, whether preliminary or definitive, or to exhibit the same publicly during the proper time and in the proper place.

(2) To any alteration of the day, hour, or place in which any public business is to be done, or to the method of its designations leading to error.

(3) To any fraudulent manipulations in matters relating to the preparation of the census, the organization of electoral boards or colleges, the voting, the resolutions or ballotings, and the nomination of candidates.

(4) To the improper and inaccurate preparation of records or documents relating to the election, or to their not being signed in the proper manner by all who should do so, or to the proper dispositions not being made of electoral records or documents.

(5) To changing or altering in the ballot which the elector deposits in the exercise of his right, or to its being hidden from public view before it is deposited in the box.

(6) To the placing of impediment or difficulty in the way of electors, candidates, or notaries in the examination of the box before voting begins, and, when the ballots are examined, in the examination of the ballots taken from the box.

(7) To the preparation of an intentionally inaccurate list, such as to obscure the truth of the names of the voters at any election.

(8) To an inaccurate counting of votes in resolutions relative to the taking or rectification of the census, or to electoral matters, and also to the inaccurate reading of ballots.

(9) To violating the secrecy of the vote or of the election with a view to influencing its results.

(10) To the issuance of an unlawful proclamation against any person.

(11) To the making of untrue statements in the verbal declaration that is to be made on the occasion of an election, or to the prevention or impeding in any way of a proper knowledge of the truth concerning the election.

(12) To the postponement of any election without grave and sufficient cause.

ART. 24. Private individuals who are directly accessory to the commission of any of the offenses enumerated in the preceding article shall be punished with the penalty of imprisonment in its minimum degree when the penal code does not impose a more serious penalty on those who are guilty of commission or omission.

ART. 25. Every act, omission, or manifestation contrary to this law or to the general provisions adopted for its execution that is not included in the foregoing articles and whose object is to restrain or exert pressure upon electors, to induce them to exercise their right, or to relinquish it against their will, shall constitute the crime of coercing voters, and if there is no more serious penalty provided for it in the penal code, it shall be punished by a fine of from 125 to 2,500 pesetas.

ART. 26. The following persons shall also be considered as committing the crime of coercing voters, although the intention of restraining or exerting pressure upon the electors may not be obvious or apparent, and shall accordingly be subject to the penalties prescribed in the foregoing article:

(1) Civil, military, or ecclesiastical authorities who advise or recommend voters to give or refuse their vote to a determinate person, and those who by the use of official means or agents, or the authorization of stamps, envelopes, seals, or notes that may have that character, recommend or advise against certain candidates.

(2) Public officers who promote or take part in the issue of Government records relating to denunciations, fines, arrears of accounts, lands, forests, granaries, or any other branch of the administration from the time when notice is given until the election is terminated.

(3) Officers, from the minister of the Crown down, who make appointments, removals, transfers, or suspensions of employees, agents, or clerks in any branch of the general, provincial, or municipal administration in the period between the giving of notice and the termination of the general balloting, when such acts are not based on legitimate reasons and affect in any way the precinct, college, district, judicial circuit, or province in which the election is held.

The cause of the removal, transfer, or suspension shall be accurately stated in the order, which shall be published in the Gazette of Madrid or in those of Havana or Puerto Rico, if it emanates from the central administration, and in the official bulletin of the respective province, if it emanates from the provincial or municipal administration. If these formalities are omitted it shall be considered as having been made without cause.

Royal decrees or orders relating to the civil governors of the provinces and to military officers shall be excepted from the above requirements. Removals, transfers, or suspensions decided upon, but of which the interested parties have not been notified before the electoral period, can not be made during said period, except in the exceptional cases and in the exceptional manner specified in this number.

ART. 27. The following persons shall be liable to the penalties provided in article 25, unless more serious ones are imposed by the penal code:

(1) Those who, by means of a promise, present, or remuneration, solicit, directly or indirectly, the vote of any elector in favor of or against any candidate.

(2) Those who incite voters to intoxication in order to obtain or secure their adhesion.

(3) Any person who votes twice or more times at an election, who takes another name in order to vote, or who votes when incapacitated or when his exercise of such right is suspended.

(4) Whoever knowingly consents, without a protest, when he might make one, to the casting of a vote in the cases mentioned in the foregoing number.

(5) Whoever prevents or delays the admission, attention to and decision concerning protests or complaints of voters, or who does not afford protection to those who make them.

(6) Whoever omits the announcements and notifications required by law, or who does not issue or cause to be issued, as speedily as the law directs, a certificate of election when application is made therefor.

(7) Whoever in any other, not provided for in this law, impedes or molests an elector in the exercise of his rights or the performance of his duty.

(8) Whoever maliciously raises or maintains, without good reason, doubts in regard to the identity of a person or the legality of his rights.

ART. 28. Public officers who cause a voter to leave his domicile or residence, or remain away from the same, even under pretext of the requirements of the public service, on the day of the election, or on a day in which he may be able and may desire to vote; or those who detain him, depriving him in similar case of his liberty, shall be liable, besides the penalties mentioned in the second paragraph of article 210 and in article 221 of the penal code, respectively, to the penalty of absolute, permanent disqualification.

ART. 29. Those who impede or hinder the free entrance and exit of the voters to and from the place in which they are to exercise their right, their approach to the voting tables, the presence of notaries, candidates, or electors in the places in which the election is to take place, in such a way as to render it impossible or difficult for them to perform their duties or exercise their right, and to verify the regularity of such elections, shall be liable, if they are public officers, to the penalty of imprisonment in its minimum degree and to a fine of 500 to 2,500 pesetas; and if they are private individuals, to the penalty of imprisonment in its minimum degree, unless other and more severe penalties are provided by the penal code, in which case the latter penalties shall be enforced.

ART. 30. Public officers who do not deliver or who maliciously delay the delivery of documents requested by special commissioners shall be punished as being guilty of the misdemeanor of serious disobedience to the authorities, without prejudice to the disciplinary responsibility which they incur at the same time.

ART. 31. Offenses provided for in the penal code, which are connected with matters relating to elections, shall be punished when the special provisions of the preceding articles are not applicable, with the penalties provided by the same code, and also with a fine of from 125 to 1,250 pesetas, in case a penalty of this class is not applicable to them.

ART. 32. The following penalties shall apply to all the offenses directly connected with the provisions of this law, whether they are provided by this or by another law: That of special disqualification, temporary or permanent, for the right of suffrage, if the guilty person is a public officer, and that of suspension from the same right if he is a private individual.

In the case of the repetition of an offense of this class the disqualification for public officers shall be absolute for all time, and for private individuals shall be absolute for a temporary period, in addition to the penalties provided.

CHAPTER II.—*Of infractions.*

ART. 33. Any failure to fulfill the obligations and formalities which this law or the provisions that shall be adopted for its execution impose upon all persons who take part in an official capacity in electoral proceedings shall be punished by a fine of from 25 to 1,000 pesetas, in case it does not constitute a crime.

Officers who, for any reason that can not be shown to be one rendering it absolutely impossible for them to do so, shall fail to perform any of the duties made incumbent upon them by this law or the regulations for its execution shall be required to pay the fine for which provision is made above, the imposition of which shall be ordered by the census board before which the duty should have been performed, due regard being had to the provisions of article 42.

The president of the provisional and municipal boards shall incur the same responsibility if, when they should receive one of the documents provided for in any of the provisions of this law or of the regulations, they shall fail to order, on their own responsibility, that it be immediately collected by a special officer at the expense of the person whose duty it was to send it.

Those who in such cases shall fail to notify the central board that they have performed this duty shall be punished in like manner.

ART. 34. The following persons shall, moreover, be punished in the manner provided by the foregoing article:

(1) Those who are present at elections and who, in some way that does not constitute a crime, disturb order, or are lacking in proper respect.

(2) Those who, not having a right to enter the electoral colleges or the ballot boards, shall not leave the place at the first intimation from the president.

(3) Those who shall enter an electoral college, section, or board with arms, sticks, canes, or umbrellas, not being officers or not being physically impeded.

(4) Notaries who, being about to perform the duties of their office, do not give previous notice of their intention to the presiding officer of the function.

(5) Officers and individuals owing to whom the proper party fails to receive, within the time fixed and in the manner provided in the law, any communication, notice, instrument, or document that should be transmitted, without prejudice to the provisions of No. 4 of article 23.

(6) Members of the census boards and their substitutes who, without just cause, shall fail to attend the sessions to which they shall have been summoned without furnishing a proper excuse.

The following shall be deemed sufficient causes for not attending the sessions:

(1) Absence from the place at which the sessions are held.

(2) Important matters connected with the public service.

(3) Matters connected with one's personal health or the health of one's family, or private business that can not be deferred.

(4) Causes in virtue of which the president or members of the central board fail to attend the meeting of that board.

CHAPTER III.—*Provisions common to the two foregoing chapters.*

ART. 35. For the purposes of this law the following persons shall be considered as public officers: Those appointed by the Government, and those who, by virtue of their office, perform any duty connected with the elections, and also the president and members of the electoral census board, and the presidents and supervisors of the ballot bureaus and boards.

ART. 36. The ordinary courts shall alone be competent to take cognizance of electoral offenses, whatever may be the personal status of the guilty parties.

For the purposes of the provisions of this title it shall be understood that the offenses specially provided for in this law are electoral offenses, and also those which, being provided for in the penal code, relate to electoral matters properly so called.

ART. 37. When any offense shall be committed in the college or electoral board the president shall order the arrest of the presumptive criminals, and shall place them at the disposal of the judicial authorities.

A penal action growing out of offenses specially electoral shall be public and, may be brought for even two months after the expiration of the term of the office conferred by the election.

For the bringing of such action no deposit or security shall be required.

Judges and courts shall proceed according to the rules governing criminal trials.

ART. 38. No authorization shall be required to bring any officer to trial.

Cases in which, by a sentence from which there is no appeal, exemption shall be granted from responsibility for due obedience, shall be referred without delay to the court that is competent to take action against the person who gave the order which has been obeyed. The term referred to in the foregoing article shall remain in abeyance with respect to the magistrate or person obeyed from the time when proceedings were first taken until the day on which the competent court shall have received the unappealable sentence in which shall be declared the exemption from responsibility of the person who has obeyed.

When the magistrate who gave the order is a minister of the Crown, or when his responsibility shall have been shown in any manner, the court taking cognizance of the case shall refer it without delay to the Congress of Deputies, when the sentence in which exemption from responsibility is declared is unappealable or the antecedents resulting therefrom indicate the responsibility of the minister.

ART. 39. The general and special provisions of the penal code shall in all cases be applicable to the offenses provided for in this law, when said provisions have reference to offenses as having been consummated, frustrated, and tentative to participation therein by the various persons who are the objects of the proceeding, to the circumstances modifying the responsibility, and to the consequent graduation and enforcement of the penalties.

H. Doc. 406——5

ART. 40. The court to which belongs the execution of unappealable decisions shall order their publication in the official bulletin of the province in which the offense shall have been committed, and shall send a copy of that newspaper to the central board.

ART. 41. No attention shall be paid by the minister of the colonies (nor shall any report thereon be made by the court or the council of state) to any application for pardon on account of electoral offenses, unless it shall previously appear that the petitioners have served at least one-half of the time for which they were sentenced to personal penalties, and have paid the full amount of the fines and costs. The authorities and members of corporations, whatever their status may be, who shall violate this provision by causing the petition for pardon to be laid before the King for decision, shall incur the responsibility provided in article 369 of the penal code.

The Government shall notify the central census board whenever a pardon is granted.

ART. 42. The punishment for infractions shall belong:

(1) To the presidents of the function or session in which they are committed.

(2) To the municipal or provincial census boards in which they are connected, respectively; with the acts of which said boards or their presidents are to take cognizance.

The municipal boards shall not, however, order any punishment in the case of superior boards, but if they understand that the provincial board has committed any infraction, they shall immediately notify the central board, that it may reach a proper decision in the matter.

When the judges fail to send to the census boards the documents which are necessary for the preparation or correction of the census, according to the regulations, said boards shall so inform the presiding judge of the proper superior court, that he may inflict the punishment, and shall send a report thereof to the central board.

(3) To the central board, the rest.

The imposition of fines shall take place in pursuance of a written decision in which the grounds therefor shall be stated. Those imposed in pursuance of the provisions of paragraph 1 of this article or by the municipal board may be appealed from before the provincial board within two days following the notification, which board shall confine itself to affirming or annulling the decision.

The rescissory decisions of the provincial board and those of that board in the exercise of its own powers may be appealed from within the same term to the central board, which may increase, diminish, and approve, or remit the fine within the limit of its powers.

ART. 43. Presidents of electoral colleges or of boards for counting votes, municipal boards and the presidents thereof, shall not impose a fine exceeding 100 pesetas (francs).

Presidents of provincial boards, and those boards, may impose a fine to the amount of 500 pesetas.

The central board and its president may impose a fine to the amount of 1,000 pesetas.

ART. 44. The payment of these fines shall be made in special paper which the department of public finance shall issue for the purpose and shall deliver on account to the provincial deputations, collecting thereon a duty of 20 per cent of its value. The remainder of its value shall be paid into the proper provincial treasury.

If, six days after the decision shall have been pronounced, the fine shall not have been paid, compulsion shall be used for its collection.

In case the person fined is insolvent, he shall suffer imprisonment at the rate of one day for each 5 pesetas of the fine, but this term shall not exceed 10 days when the fine shall have been imposed by the municipal board, its president, or the president of the bureau; it shall not exceed 20 days if the fine shall have been imposed by the provincial board, its president, or by the boards for counting votes, and it shall not exceed 30 days if the fine shall have been imposed by the central board or its president.

TRANSIENT PROVISIONS.

First. Within the three days following the publication of this law in the gazettes of Havana and Puerto Rico, a board shall be formed in each one of the capitals of the island, which shall be called the insular board for the electoral census. It shall be composed of the Governor-General, who shall be its president; of the governmental divisions of the superior courts of Havana and Puerto Rico, respectively; of two members, chosen by the Governor-General from among the most influential residents, to represent in the board the political parties of the island, and of the secretary of the general government, the latter to have the right of discussion, but no vote, and he shall perform the duties of secretary. Moreover, the civil governor of Havana shall be a member of the insular board for the electoral census of the Island of Cuba.

The powers of these boards shall be:

(1) To inspect and direct all services connected with the preparation and preservation of the census.

(2) To preserve the printed copies of the final lists which shall have been taken from the provincial registers.

(3) To communicate, through the president, with all public authorities and officers.

(4) To receive and decide all complaints that are addressed to them.

(5) To exercise disciplinary jurisdiction over all persons taking part, officially, in electoral operations, imposing fines to the amount of 1,000 pesetas, which, the case arising, shall be collected by their order, by judges of first instance.

(6) To settle questions that may arise in connection with the execution of this law and its regulations, adapting the provisions of both to the condition of the island so as to secure independence and a genuine vote.

The insular board of Cuba shall, moreover, issue such orders as it may think proper, for the holding of elections in those districts in which the state of the insurrection shall not permit the taking of the electoral census in time, or to hold such elections according to the provisions of this law and the regulations for its execution. For this purpose each of the districts in question shall appoint delegates who, together with seven of the largest taxpayers on agricultural and manufacturing property, and seven capacities (?) shall proceed to hold the election, according to such instruction as may be communicated to them by the insular board.

Second. In execution of the provisions of article 4 of this law, before the 26th day of December next, the presiding judges of the superior courts shall appoint the magistrates who are to preside over the provincial electoral census boards, and the officers who are to preside over the municipal boards in those localities in which there are no judges of first instance.

Third. In order that the elections may be held as speedily as possible, and the new political and administrative officers may perform their functions in the islands of Cuba and Puerto Rico, the following shall be the mode of procedure:

On the 1st day of January, 1898, at 8 o'clock a. m., the president of the municipal electoral census board, having been appointed by the superior court of the province, shall proceed, in the hall of sessions of the municipal district, and in public session, to organize said municipal board in the manner provided in Art. 4 of this law.

The alcalde shall then state the result of the last census, and shall deliver to the president of the board a duplicate list, in alphabetical order, and with correlative numbering of all the inhabitants above 25 years of age whose names appear in said census, in which shall be stated their ages, residences, and occupations, and whether they are able to read and write. All the sheets belonging to this list shall be signed by the alcalde and the secretary of the municipal board.

The president on his own responsibility shall immediately cause one of the copies of this list to be posted in the usual place for municipal edicts and proclamations, and shall at the same time make known by a proclamation or through the crier that, on the 5th of the aforesaid month of January, at 8 a. m., the municipal census board shall meet in public session in the hall of sessions of the municipal board.

Before the said 5th day of January the judges of first instance shall send to the presidents of the respective municipal census boards a certified list of the judicial decisions which affect the electoral capacity of the inhabitants of each municipal district, and the municipal judges shall send a list, likewise certified, of the aforesaid inhabitants who shall have died since the date of the last quinquennial census.

On the 5th day of January, the municipal board shall organize, in public session, at the time and in the place aforesaid, and the president shall lay on the table the list of residents prepared by the alcalde, the last census, and the certificates sent in by the judges.

The board shall hear all representations that shall be made concerning enrollments, exclusions, and corrections. For claims with regard to enrollment it shall be sufficient to furnish evidence by means of two witnesses that the person whose enrollment in the list is desired possesses the requisites that are legally required to make him an elector.

The public session being terminated, the junta shall proceed to the preparation of the following lists:

1. A list of all the inhabitants who possess the right to vote, according to the census list.

2. A list of those who have died since said list was prepared according to the data furnished by the respective municipal judges.

3. A list of those who are disqualified.

These lists shall be published as provided for in the first paragraph of this resolution, for the three following days, during which time an appeal may be taken to the provincial board.

In the same session the municipal board shall order the division of the voters of the municipal district into sections if their number shall exceed 500, assigning to each section a number approximately equal, according to the conditions of each locality.

This having been done, a copy shall be made in duplicate from the first list in alphabetical order of the names of the voters of each municipal district, divided into sections, and these copies shall constitute the final lists. On the 9th of January one of them shall be transmitted, together with a certificate of the order for the division of the municipal district into sections, and of the complaints which have been presented, to the provincial census board, which shall adopt such decisions as it may think proper, making the proper modifications for the case arising, and shall cause to be printed in the Boletin the lists of the voters of the province before the 20th of January.

A printed copy of the list for each municipal district, authorized by the president and secretary of the provincial board, shall be transmitted, certified, the leaves being all under seal, to the respective president of the municipal board, who shall inform the board, and who shall cause to be posted in a public place for three days, a copy of that document, which shall be placed in the archives. The president and secretary of the junta shall be responsible for the absolute correctness of this copy.

Similar copies shall also be transmitted by the president of the provincial board to the authorities that are declared by the regulations to be entitled to receive them.

There shall be no appeal from the decisions adopted by the provincial boards in virtue of this temporary provision, excepting a complaint to the insular board.

The day previous to that appointed for the first elections to be held after the promulgation of this law the municipal census boards shall meet and order the enrollment in the electoral lists of those who have applied for it up to that date who have the testimony of two witnesses to show that they possess the conditions which this law requires in order that they may vote.

Those enrolled by virtue of these orders or by the decisions of the insular board shall exercise their right in the section in which they are domiciled.

Fourth. Until a new division shall have been made in the electoral districts for deputies to the Cortes in the territory of the islands of Cuba and Puerto Rico, the one now existing shall remain in force.

The insular electoral census boards shall divide the territory of the islands into districts and sections for the election of representatives, pursuant to the royal decree of this date.

Approved by Her Majesty. SAGASTA.
MADRID, *November 25, 1897.*

Articles of the electoral law of the Peninsula of June 26, 1890, in the form in which they are to be enforced, according to article 13 of the law of Cuba and Puerto Rico.

ART. 4. The following are indispensable requirements for admission as a deputy to the congress:

1. To possess the qualifications required by article 29 of the constitution on the day on which the election in the electoral district is held.
2. To have been elected and declared elected in an electoral district, or in the congress, in accordance with the provisions of this law and those of the regulations of that body.
3. Not to be disqualified by any reason of personal incapacity for holding the office on the day on which the election is held.
4. Not to be included in any of the cases established by the law concerning disqualifications.

ART. 5. Disqualified for admission as deputies, although validly elected, are:

1. Those found to be included in any of the cases mentioned in article 2 of this law. The rehabilitation mentioned in No. 2 of article 2 of this law must be secured for the eligibility of a deputy at least two years previous to his election.
2. Contractors for works or public services paid for out of the general funds of the province or municipality; those who, as the result of such contracts, have claims pending in their own interest against the administration and in the sureties and partners of such contractors. This incapacity is to be understood as relating solely to the district or section in which the work or public service is performed.
3. Those who fill, or have filled within a year, in the district or section in which the election is held, any office, charge, or commission, by appointment of the Government, or who have exercised authority in a popular election, among whom are included presidents of deputations, and deputies who, during the previous year, have been members of provincial commissions.

Excepted from this are the ministers of the Crown and officers of the central administration of the islands and of the peninsula.

The disqualifications referred to in No. 3 are confined to the votes cast in the district or section or within the limit of the authority or functions with which the deputy has been invested.

ART. 6. When a deputy shall become disqualified after admission to the congress from any of the causes enumerated in Art. 5, his incapacity shall be declared and he shall immediately forfeit his office.

ART. 7. Those who already hold the office of deputy to the cortes shall not be admitted to the same congress by virtue of a partial election unless they have resigned the same before notice has been given to the district of such partial election.

ART. 8. The office of deputy to the cortes is gratuitous and voluntary, and may be resigned before and after taking the oath of office; but no resignation shall be admissible without the previous approval by the congress of the deputy's certificate of election.

ART. 22. In districts in which a deputy is to be elected no elector shall have the right to vote for more than one person; when more than one and as many as four are to be elected he shall have the right to vote for one less than the number to be elected; for two less if more than four are to be elected, and for three less if more than eight are to be elected.

ART. 37. The following candidates shall have the right to appoint supervisors for the electoral bureaus of the precincts comprising the district or section:

1. Ex-deputies to the Cortes, who have represented the same district or any other on the island.
2. Those who have been candidates in the same district in former elections and obtained at least one-fifth of all the votes cast.
3. Ex-senators elected by the island to which the district or section belongs.
4. Candidates for the office of deputy to the Cortes, proposed by means of tickets signed by electors of the respective district or section, or by notarial instruments, in the preparation of which a competent officer has taken part, the number of such electors being equal to at least one-twentieth of the entire number of those included in the final list of the district or section.

ART. 73. Only in pursuance of a resolution of Congress shall it be possible to proceed to a partial election for deputy in one or more districts, or because the post of representative of such district or districts has become vacant.

ART. 74. For the districts which, according to this law, are to elect three or more deputies, it shall be understood that there is a vacancy in their representation in the Cortes only when, for any reason, at least two deputies fail to act as such.

ART. 75. The royal decree convoking the electoral colleges of one or more districts for the partial election of deputies to the Cortes shall be published in the Gaceta de Madrid within eight days, reckoned from the date of the communication of the resolution of Congress. In the said royal decree the day shall be fixed on which the election shall take place, and that day shall not be fixed before twenty or after thirty days, reckoned from the date of the convocation. The royal decree shall be simultaneously published in the gazettes of Havana and Puerto Rico, according to circumstances, the proper order being communicated for that purpose by telegraph to the respective governors-general of the two Antilles.

ART. 76. The partial election shall take place on the day appointed, according to the procedure and in the form prescribed by this law for general elections.

ART. 77. Congress, exercising the prerogative belonging to it according to article 34 of the constitution, shall examine and judge of the legality of the elections according to the procedure provided by its regulations, and shall admit as deputies those who are found to have been legally elected and proclaimed in the districts, if they possess the capacity necessary to enable them to discharge the duties of the office, and are not disqualified in any of the ways defined by law.

ART. 78. In the case of an election in which the votes for each candidate are equal in number, if only one of the candidates who have received the same number of votes shall possess legal fitness to be deputy he shall at once be proclaimed and admitted, provided that the election is approved.

He who is shown to be legally elected shall likewise be at once admitted and proclaimed by Congress if there shall be, in the certificate of election, protests which seem justified against the votes cast for the other one or more candidates having an equal number of votes.

If there are no such differences, that one of the candidates having an equal number of votes shall be proclaimed deputy who—
(1) Has most frequently filled the office;
(2) Who has filled it for the longest time;
(3) Who is the oldest in years.

ART. 79. The certificates of the ballot board having been sent to the central board, agreeably to the provisions of article 69, shall be delivered by the latter, as they come into his possession, at the office of the secretary of Congress, at whose disposal that board shall, in all cases, hold the other documents relating to certificates of election.

ART. 80. The deputies elect or presumptive, who have proclaimed by the examining boards (ballot boards) at general elections, shall present their respective credentials within two months, reckoning from the day of the meeting of the Cortes. For those proclaimed elected at partial elections the time shall be reckoned from the day of their proclamation by the examining board (ballot board). It shall be understood that he who does not present his credentials within the period fixed by this article resigns his office, and, consequently, a vacancy in the district or college concerned shall be declared after Congress shall have decided concerning the legality of the election.

ART. 81. If the same individual shall be found to have been elected by two or more districts at the same time, he shall make choice before Congress of one of them within eight days after the last of his certificates of election shall have been approved, if he shall then have been admitted as a deputy, or within thirty days if otherwise.

In default of a choice within either term, the district that belongs to him shall be decided by lot in Congress, and a vacancy shall be declared with respect to the others.

ART. 82. The electors and the candidates who have taken part or been concerned in an election may have recourse to Congress at any time before the approval of the respective certificates of election with such complaints as they may desire to present with regard to the validity or result of such election, or with regard to the legal qualifications of the deputy elect previous to his having been admitted.

ART. 83. When, in order to be able to appreciate and judge of the legality of an election concerning which complaint is made before Congress, it shall be thought necessary to make some negotiations in the locality where such election was held, the president of the chamber shall give and directly communicate orders to the judicial magistrate of the territory whom he may think proper to commission for the purpose, and the commissioned magistrate shall consult with the said President in the performance of his duty without any necessity for the intervention of the Government.

ART. 84. After an election has been approved by Congress and the deputy elected by it has been admitted, no complaint shall be received, nor shall any subsequent discussion be permitted respecting the validity of the said election, or regarding the legal fitness of the deputy, unless on account of incapacity that has occurred since his admission.

Approved by Her Majesty.

SAGASTA.

MADRID, *November 25, 1897.*

[From the Gaceta de Madrid, Saturday, November 27, 1897.]

OFFICIAL.—PRESIDENT OF THE COUNCIL OF MINISTERS.

STATEMENT.

MADAM: In endeavoring to solve the problem of introducing colonial autonomy into the islands of Cuba and Puerto Rico, which task, together with that of the pacification of the territory of Cuba, constitutes the engagements which the Government has contracted with the nation, the ministers think that detailed explanations and comments on the complex matters embraced in the plan should give way to a temperate but full statement of its fundamental character, or of the spheres of action to which it extends and of the consequences which, in their opinion, must be the result of the régime which they propose to Your Majesty for the government of the Spanish Antilles.

Criticism and analysis will speedily elucidate all that relates to the details; the essential ideas and the inspiration of the decree have their appropriate place here and at this time only.

This is the more necessary since the first and most essential condition of success in reforms of this kind is absolute sincerity of purpose. With this sincerity the Government has examined the best form of an autonomic constitution for the islands of Cuba and Puerto Rico, and it hopes clearly to demonstrate, in these observations, that the intention and the results have gone hand in hand.

It was proposed, in the first place, clearly to establish the principle, to develop it in its entirety, and to surround it with every guaranty of success, because, when it is sought to intrust the direction of affairs to peoples that have reached the age of virility, either no mention of autonomy should be made to them or it should be given to them complete, with the conviction that they are started on the right road with the restrictions or shackles which are born of distrust and suspicion. Either the defense of nationality is confided to repression and force or it is turned over to a reconciliation of affection and tradition with interest, and this reconciliation is strengthened according as it is developed by the advantages of a system of government that teaches and gives evidence to the colonies that under no other will it be possible for them to attain a higher degree of welfare, security, and greatness.

This being the case, it was a condition essential to the attainment of the purpose had in view to seek for that principle a practical form and one that was intelligible to the people that had to be governed by it, and the Government found this in the programme of that insular party, considerable in numbers, but still more important by reason of its intelligence and perseverance, the predictions of which party have, for twenty years past, made the people of Cuba familiar with the spirit, the procedure and the great importance of the serious innovation which they are called upon to introduce into their political and social life.

It is asserted by the foregoing that the project is in nowise theoretical, and that it is not an imitation or copy of other colonial constitutions which have been justly regarded as models in the matter, for although the Government has carefully considered what those instruments teach it realizes that the institutions of peoples which, in their history and their race, differ so much from that of Cuba, can not take root where they have neither precedent nor atmosphere, nor that preparation which is the outgrowth of education and belief.

The problem having been thus defined, inasmuch as the question was to give an autonomic constitution to a Spanish territory peopled by a Spanish race and civilized by Europe, there was no longer any doubt as to the decision to be reached; autonomy had to be developed according to the ideas and the programme which bears that name in the Antilles, without eliminating anything of its contents, and especially without altering its spirit, but rather by completing and harmonizing it and giving it greater guaranties of stability, as should be done by the government of a mother country which feels itself called to establish such a programme, from a conviction of its advantages, from a desire to carry peace and tranquillity to those highly prized territories, and from a consciousness of its own responsibility, not only to the colonies, but also to its own vast interests which time has connected and woven together in the impenetrable net of years.

Being thus sure of the form which best fitted its design, the Government found it easy to distinguish the three aspects offered by the establishment of an autonomic constitution. In the first place, the sacred interests or the mother country, which, being alarmed and distrustful on account of the course pursued by many of her sons, and wounded by the ingratitude of those who put more trust in the selfishness of the speculator than they do in brotherly affection, desires above all things that the change for which she is prepared should draw closer and strengthen the bond of sovereignty, and that in the midst of a blessed peace the interests of all her sons, which are not at variance with each other, although they may be at times different, should be harmonized and developed by the free consent of all.

Next are to be considered the aspirations, the needs, and the desires of our colonial population, which is anxious to be treated like an unfortunate daughter instead of being crushed like an enemy, which is obedient to the call of affection, and ready to rebel like Spaniards against the brutal imposition of exterminating force. These people expect from the mother country a form in which their initiative may be molded and a mode of procedure that may authorize them to manage their own interests.

And finally, this vast and interesting mass of relations created of interests developed in that long past which nobody, still less a Government, is at liberty to disregard or forget, and whose preservation and development involve the fulfillment of the destiny of our race in America, and the glory of the Spanish flag in lands that were discovered and civilized by our ancestors.

These three orders of ideas find their answer in the fundamental provisions of the draft submitted to your Majesty for approval. To the first, that is, to the point of view of the mother country, belong the questions of sovereignty which have been confided to the highest authorities of the Spanish nation. The representation and authority of the King, who is the nation itself, the command of the army and navy, the administration of justice, diplomatic understanding with America, the constant and beneficent relations between the colony and the mother country, the pardoning power and the upholding and defense of the constitution are intrusted to the Governor-General as the King's representative, and under the direction of the council of ministers. Nothing that is essential has been forgotten; the authority of the central power is in nowise diminished or abated.

The insular aspect is, in its turn, developed in a manner as full and complete as could be desired by those who are most exacting, in central, provincial, and municipal autonomy; in the application without reserve or equivocation of the parliamentary system; in the powers of the insular chambers and in the creation of a responsible government, at the head of which, and forming the supreme bond of nationality as regards the executive power, again appears the Governor-General who, on the one hand, presides through responsible ministers over the development of colonial life, and, on the other, associates and connects it with the general life of the nation.

And that third aspect, in which is recapitulated the history of the relations between the Antilles and the mother country, and within which their commerce, their credit, and their wealth, must also be developed, is defined in a series of provisions of a permanent character, which connects the two executive powers—the insular and the national, and at times, their chambers—in such a manner that at every moment they lend each other mutual aid, and assist each other in developing the common interests.

And all this manifold and complex, though not complicated, system is sanctioned and rendered practical by a series of guaranties of associations of constant understandings and public discussions which will absolutely prevent, so far as it is allowable for man to predict that which is to come, unyielding dilemmas, insurmountable difficulties, and collisions between the colonies and the mother country.

This is a point of so great importance that the Government would certainly have subordinated all other questions to it if such subordination had been necessary, which it can not be, nor is there any reason to fear it, since the bases of the new régime are established upon harmony of interests, scrupulous respect for the rights of others, and the desire in the mother country unremittingly to aid the development, prosperity, and peaceful aggrandizement of her beautiful Antilles, which desire the Government does not doubt will be fully shared there.

This does not mean that no questions will arise in which the two spheres of action will be confounded, and that there will be no legitimate doubts as to which is the predominant interest in them, or that there will not be, after the doubts, more or less of passionate discussion. In no colony enjoying autonomy has this failed to happen; in none has the case arisen in which the central Government was always and systematically in accord with the acts of the colonial government. Long is the list of the legislative enactments of Canada which have been vetoed by the British Government, and curious and exceedingly interesting is the list of judicial decisions which have defined the diverse jurisdictions of their local assemblies, either among themselves or with their governors. This has been the case notwithstanding the fact that tho great decentralization, the antecedents of Canadian history, and freedom of trade greatly simplify the relations between the two countries.

The excellence of the system, however, lies in the fact that when such cases arise, and especially when they are frequent, the balance of power both within the colonial constitution and in the relations of the colony to the mother country is such that a remedy is always to be had, that a basis of understanding is never lacking, and that a common ground is always to be found on which interests are either harmonized or their antagonism is settled or the will of the people bows to the decision of the courts.

If, therefore, the rights which are recognized by the constitution as belonging to the citizens are violated or their interests are disregarded by the town boards and deputations which are, in their turn, within the system, entirely autonomous, the courts of justice will defend and uphold them; if corporations go beyond their powers, or if, on the other hand, the executive power undertakes to impair what the constitution of the kingdom or the provisions of this decreo declare to be powers belonging to the town boards or the provincial corporations, the accused party has the right to appeal to the courts of the island, and as a last resort to the supreme court, whose duty it will be to settle disputes of jurisdiction between the Governor-General and the colonial parliament, whoever may have given rise to such disputes; both will have the same rights to complain and to seek legal redress for their wrongs.

Thus, whatever difficulties may arise from the establishment of a system, or be the outgrowth of its exercise, will be decided by the courts, which have been, since ancient Rome down to modern England, the most progressive source of right, and which have afforded the most flexible procedure for the harmonization of the growing demands of real life and the slow process of legislation.

Thus the autonomic constitution which the Government proposes for the islands of Cuba and Puerto Rico is not exotic or copied, nor is it an imitation. It is an organization *sui generis*, conceived and upheld by the natives of the Spanish Antilles, gladly inscribed by the liberal party in their programme in order that the nation might know what it had to expect from that party when it should come into power, and characterized by a feature which no colonial régime has thus far presented, viz: that the Antilles can be wholly autonomous, in the fullest sense of the word, and at the same time have their representatives and form a part of the national parliament.

So that, while the representatives of the insular people direct from their local chambers the special interests of their country, others elected by the same people aid and cooperate in the Cortes in the making of those laws in whose mould are formed and unified the different elements of Spanish nationality. And this is not a small or paltry advantage; still less does it furnish ground for surprise, as some might, perhaps, think, because this present of the deputies from the Antilles in the

Cortes is a close bond of the nationality which is raised above all the unities which live in its bosom, now sought as one of the greatest political steps in advance of our day by the autonomous English colonies, which are anxious to take part in an Imperial Parliament in the supreme function of legislators and directors of the great British Empire.

This form, therefore, which is characteristic of the system now adopted by Spain, while it gives it its own meaning, signifies, if not a step in advance, such as those engendered by the present time, an advantage which circumstances offer us as a just compensation for the immense disasters which our colonial history recounts.

The Government frankly acknowledges that for the success of its work public discussion in Parliament would have been better, together with the analysis of public opinion in the press, on the lecture platform, and in books; but it is not its fault, as it was not that of the previous Government, if the pressure of circumstances compels it to do without this precious guaranty. Yet if the party which now serves the interests of the Crown and the country in the Government did not hesitate a moment to approve, in its day, the initiative taken by the conservative party, or in voting for the appropriation which it asked from the Cortes, it has a right, now that the weight of circumstances is still heavier than it was then, to hope that public opinion will approve to-day the course pursued by it, and that the Cortes will do so to-morrow.

For this reason it does not hesitate to face the responsibility, and it intends to put into immediate action and practice the solutions which are implied in the present decree with the same sincerity with which it has prepared it, thus removing the suspicion of any indecision in its course or of reservations in its promises. If the régime shall be found wanting in practice for lack of good faith in anybody it will never be—and we are proud to proclaim this—the fault of the men who are actuated above all things by the noble desire to pacify their country.

The Government thinks that it has thus said everything necessary to make known the genesis, the inspiration, and the character of the plan which, establishing in Cuba and Puerto Rico an autonomic régime, it now submits to Your Majesty.

To those who are familiar with the constitution of the Monarchy, the plan will certainly not present any great difficulties, for the Government has, as far as possible, taken for its guide the organic system of that instrument, the division of its titles, and even its wording. The modifications of the constitutional articles are accessory and circumstantial; the additions respond to its specialty and seek to secure the efficiency of its provisions and the facility of their execution.

Doubtless something will remain to be done, and some reforms will be needed; this will be shown simultaneously by the defense of its provisions and the criticisms made thereon, and gradually the good grounds upon which both are based will be ascertained; this will render it possible to incorporate what is good in the plan and to reject what does not harmonize with its fundamental ideas when the time comes for it to receive the sanction of the Cortes.

Let it be understood, nevertheless, that the Government will not eliminate from it, nor will it consent that anything be eliminated that goes to form colonial liberties, guarantees, and privileges, because being prepared to complete its work or to throw light upon doubts, it does not intend that when it presents its plan for parliamentary sanction the concessions made shall suffer any impairment, nor can it consent to do so if it has a majority in the chambers.

But though all that the Government considers necessary to explain in the general lines of the decree has been set forth in the foregoing, it still deems it indispensable, for reasons which will readily be understood, to fix the sense of the articles which refer to autonomy with regard to the tariff, and which refer to the debt which burdens the Cuban treasury.

The export trade from the Peninsula to Cuba, which amounts to about $30,000,000 per annum, and which, moreover, furnishes ground for important combinations for navigation on the high seas, has hitherto been subjected to an exceptional régime which is absolutely incompatible with the principle of colonial autonomy.

This implies the power to regulate the conditions of its import and export trade and to have free control of its custom-houses. To refuse these privileges to Cuba or Puerto Rico would be tantamount to nullifying the value of the principles laid down; to endeavor to defeat their object would be incompatible with the dignity of the nation. What it behooves the Government to do, after recognizing the principle in its entirety, is to endeavor to cause the transition to take place without violence or injury to the interests which have been developed under the old system, and for this purpose to pave the way to an understanding with the governments of the Antilles.

The most earnest advocates of autonomy have never denied the willingness of those countries to recognize, in behalf of genuinely national industry and commerce, a margin that should secure that market to them.

This assurance has always been given by their representatives in the Cortes, and is still given by their representatives in the Cortes, and is still given by all parties in the Island of Cuba, according to statements which the Government considers irrecusable.

Complaints arose, not from the existence of discriminating duties, but from the fact that those duties were too high, and that this prevented the Antilles from securing the markets which they needed for their rich and abundant productions, and from the lack of reciprocity. Thus, as no insurmountable difficulties exist, there is ground for saying that an understanding is more than possible; that it is certain, especially when it is considered that the exports from the peninsula to Cuba consist of about fifty articles of the four hundred that are specified in the tariff, and that of these fifty many, owing to their special character, and owing to the customs and tastes of the Cubans, will never have reason to fear the competition of foreign articles.

The manufacturers and shipowners of the Peninsula have no cause for alarm owing to the establishment of a system of autonomy, which, while it modifies the conditions on which the tariff is based, does not alter the essential bases of the economic relations between Spain and the Antilles. There will doubtless be some difficulties to be harmonized, or it will be necessary to settle the inevitable differences accompanying any change of the mercantile régime; it will be necessary to combine both tariffs in some way; but neither are the interests of Cuba opposed to those of the Peninsula, nor is it to any one's interest to diminish the commercial relations existing between the two countries.

If then the insular government were already established, and if with it it had been possible to agree upon a system of mercantile relations, this question would not have assumed proportions which it does not possess; nor would there be any cause for predicting ruin and disaster; the facts would put suppositions to silence. Notwithstanding this, the Government has thought that in order to quiet alarm, it was proper for it to anticipate events, and that instead of leaving the settlement of the question to the natural working of the new constitution, it was proper to fix without further delay the bases of our future mercantile relations. In doing this and with a view to removing all cause of distrust, it has gone so far as to fix a maximum for the differential duties that are to be obtained by peninsular goods, offering, as was right and just, the same rates to insular productions.

The basis of the understanding having been fixed and determined, the principle of autonomy having been guaranteed, the equality of powers having been established in an unquestionable manner in the procedure that is to be observed, and the spirit which actuates those islanders being known, the negotiation will be easy and its results will be advantageous to both parties.

As to the debt which burdens the Cuban treasury, either directly or owing to the guarantee which it has given to that of the Peninsula, and which the latter bears analogously, the justice of dividing it in an equitable manner when the termination of the war shall render it possible to fix its definitive amount is not to be doubted for a moment.

This debt, let us hope, will not be so enormous as to amount to an insupportable burden upon the energy of the nation, nor is the nation so lacking in resources that it needs to feel alarm at the prospect before it. A country which during the past few months has given such strong evidence of virility and social discipline; a territory like that of Cuba, which, even in the midst of its political convulsions and of war scarcely interrupted for thirty years, has produced so great wealth by cultivating only a small part of its fertile soil, and which has done this by its own strength alone, with few institutions of credit, struggling against sugar on which a bounty is paid, the American market being closed to its manufactured tobacco, and at the same time changing slave labor into free labor, may calmly contemplate the payment of its obligations and inspire its creditors with confidence.

Consequently, in the opinion of the Government, it is important to think from this time forward of the manner in which the debt is to be paid, rather than of its division, applying the economic methods of our day to the great wealth which the soil of Cuba secures to agriculturists and which the bowels of the earth secure to miners, and taking advantage of the extraordinary facilities offered to the commerce of the world by the insular form and the geographical situation of what has rightly been called the "Pearl of the Antilles."

If no legislation can yet be enacted concerning these things, it is proper to bear them in mind very carefully and to pay much attention to them, since it has occurred to others who certainly can not be charged with being visionary or forming illusions—it has occurred to them, I say, to take advantage of this great germ of wealth, not, indeed, for the benefit of Spain or to uphold her sovereignty; when they do this, it would be fooling not to follow their example and not to convert into a redemption of the past and a guaranty of the future what has perhaps been an incentive to war and the origin in a great measure of the evils which we are now so eagerly seeking to remedy.

Basing its action on these considerations, the Government has the honor to submit the inclosed draft of a decree to Your Majesty for approval.

Madam, at Your Majesty's royal feet,

PRÁXEDES MATEO SAGASTA.

MADRID, *November 25, 1897.*

ROYAL DECREE.

By the advice and consent of my council of ministers. In the name of my august son, King Alfonso XIII, and as Queen Regent of the Kingdom, I decree as follows:

TITLE I.—*Of the government and administration of the islands of Cuba and Puerto Rico.*

ARTICLE I. The islands of Cuba and Puerto Rico shall hereafter be governed and administered in accordance with the following provisions:

Explanatory note.

To facilitate the understanding of this decree and to prevent confusion as regards the legal value of the terms therein used the following definitions must be remembered:
Executive central power: The King with his council of ministers.
Spanish Parliament: The Cortes with the King.
Spanish Chambers: The Congress and the Senate.
Central Government: The council of ministers of the Kingdom.
Colonial parliament: The two chambers with the Governor-General.
Colonial chambers: The council of administration and the chamber of representatives.
Colonial legislative assemblies: The council of administration and the chamber of representatives.
Governor-General in council: The Governor-General, with his secretaries.
Instructions of the Governor-General: Those which he received when he was appointed to his post.
Statute: Colonial provision of a legislative character.
Colonial statutes: The colonial legislation.
Legislation or general laws: The legislation or laws of the Kingdom.

ART. 2. The government of each one of the islands shall be composed of an insular parliament, divided into two chambers, and of a governor-general representing the mother-country, who, in the name of the latter, shall exercise supreme authority.

TITLE II.—*Of the insular chambers.*

ART. 3. The insular chambers, together with the governor-general, shall have power to legislate concerning colonial affairs in the manner and on the terms provided by law.

ART. 4. The islands shall be represented by two bodies, whose power shall be equal, viz: The chamber of representatives and the council of administration.

ART. 5. The council shall be composed of 35 members, of whom 18 shall be elected in the manner prescribed in the electoral law, and the remaining 17 shall be designated by the King, and in his name by the governor-general, from among those possessing the requirements enumerated in the following articles:

ART. 6. To be entitled to a seat in the council of administration it shall be necessary to be a Spaniard; to have attained the age of 35 years; to have been born in the island, or to have resided there uninterruptedly for four years; not to be under criminal prosecution; to be in the full enjoyment of one's political rights; not to have one's property embargoed; to have had for two or more years an income of one's own amounting to $4,000, and to have no part in contracts with the central government or with that of the island.

Stockholders in joint-stock companies shall not be considered as having a contract with the government, although the society to which they belong may have one.

ART. 7. Those who, in addition to the requirements mentioned in the foregoing article, possess any one of the following, may be elected or designated as members of the council of administration:

(1) Being or having been a senator of the Kingdom, or having the requirements specified in Title III of the constitution for the discharge of the duty of that office.

(2) Having discharged for two years the duties of one of the offices mentioned below:

That of presiding judge of the superior court of Havana, or of the Government attorney attached to that court; that of rector of the University of Havana; that of a member of the old council of administration; president of the chamber of commerce of the capital; president of the Economic Society of Friends of the Country, of Havana; president of the Club of Landholders; president of the Tobacco Manufacturers' Union; president of the League of Merchants, Manufacturers, and Agriculturists of Cuba; dean of the Illustrious College of Lawyers, of the capital; alcalde of Havana; president of its provincial deputation for two terms of two years each, or president of a provincial deputation for three such terms; dean of any of the cathedral cabildos.

(3) The following persons may likewise be elected or designated: Land owners whose names appear in the list of the 50 largest taxpayers on land held by them, or in that of the first 50 for trade, professions, industry, and arts.

ART. 8. The appointment of the members of the council whom the Crown may designate shall take place by special decrees, in which the ground on which the appointment is based shall always be stated.

The members of the council thus appointed shall hold their office during life.

One-half of the elective members of the council shall be renewed every five years, and all shall be renewed whenever the Governor-General shall dissolve the council of administration.

ART. 9. The requirements necessary to be appointed or elected councilor of administration may be changed by a law of the kingdom at the request or in accordance with the suggestion of the insular chambers.

ART. 10. Members of the council of administration shall accept no office and no title or decoration while the sessions last, but both the local and the central government may confer upon them, within their respective office or categories, such commissions as the public service may require.

The office of secretary of the government shall be excepted from the provisions contained in the foregoing paragraphs.

TITLE IV.—*Of the chamber of representatives.*

ART. 11. The chamber of representatives shall be composed of the persons named by the electoral boards in the manner provided by law and in the proportion of one to every 25,000 inhabitants.

ART. 12. In order to be elected a representative it is necessary to be a Spaniard, not in clerical orders, of full age, to be in the enjoyment of all one's civil rights, to have been born in the Island of Cuba, or to have resided there for four years, and not to be under a criminal prosecution.

ART. 13. Representatives shall be elected for five years, and may be reelected indefinitely.

The insular chamber shall decide with what functions the office of representative is incompatible, and shall determine in what cases a representative may be reelected.

ART. 14. Representatives upon whom the central or local government shall confer a pension, an office, a promotion out of the regular course, a commission with salary, honors or decorations, shall cease to hold their office, without the necessity of any declaration if, within the fifteen days immediately following their appointment, they do not inform the chamber that they decline to accept the favor conferred.

What is contained in the foregoing paragraph does not include representatives who are appointed government secretaries.

TITLE V.—*Of the manner in which the insular chambers are to perform their functions, and of the relations between them both.*

ART. 15. The chambers shall meet every year. It shall be the duty of the King, and in his name of the Governor-General, to convoke or suspend them, to close their sessions, and to dissolve separately or simultaneously the chamber of representatives and the council of administration, with the obligation to convoke them again or to renew them within three months.

ART. 16. Each one of the colegislative bodies shall draw up its own regulations and shall examine both the qualifications of the persons who compose them and the legality of their election.

Until the chamber of representatives and the council of administration shall have approved their regulations, they shall be governed by the regulations of the congress of deputies or by those of the senate, respectively.

ART. 17. Both chambers shall choose their president, vice-presidents, and secretaries.

ART. 18. One of the two legislative bodies shall not be in session unless the other is also.

The case is excepted in which the council of administration shall perform judicial functions.

ART. 19. The insular chambers shall not deliberate together or in presence of the Governor-General.

Their sessions shall be public, although in cases in which secrecy is required each one may hold a secret session.

ART. 20. It shall be the duty of the Governor-General, through the governmental secretaries, just as it shall be that of each one of the two chambers, to initiate and propose the colonial statutes.

ART. 21. The colonial statutes concerning taxes and public credit shall be first laid before the chamber of representatives.

ART. 22. Resolutions in each one of the co-legislative bodies shall be taken by a plurality of votes; but in order to pass enactments of a legislative character, the presence of one-half plus one of the total number of members composing it shall be required. The presence of one-third of the members shall, however, be sufficient for deliberation.

ART. 23. In order that a resolution may be understood to have been passed by the insular parliament, it shall be necessary for it to have been approved both by the chamber of representatives and by the council of administration.

ART. 24. The colonial statutes, when approved in the manner provided in the foregoing article, shall be laid before the Governor-General by the officers of the respective chambers for his sanction and promulgation.

ART. 25. The members of the council of administration and those of the chamber of representatives shall be inviolable as regards their opinions and votes in the discharge of the duties of their office.

ART. 26. The members of the council of administration shall not be prosecuted or arrested without a previous resolution of the council, unless when they are taken in flagrante delicto or when the council is not in session; but in all cases a report shall be made to that body as speedily as possible, in order that it may reach a proper determination. The representatives shall, moreover, not be prosecuted or arrested during the sessions of the chamber without its permission, unless they are taken in flagrante delicto; but in this case, and in that of their being prosecuted or arrested when the chambers are closed, a report shall be made as speedily as possible to the chamber of representatives, for its information and decision.

The superior court of Havana shall take cognizance of criminal cases against members of the council and representatives, in such cases and in such manner as the colonial statutes provide.

ART. 27. The guarantees provided in the foregoing article shall not be applicable to cases in which a member of the council or a representative shall declare that he is the author of articles, books, pamphlets, or printed matter of any kind in which soldiers are incited to sedition, or in which the Governor-General is insulted or slandered, or an attack is made upon the national integrity.

ART. 28. The relations between the two chambers shall be regulated, until further orders, by the law concerning the relations between both colegislative bodies bearing date of July 19, 1837.

ART. 29. In addition to holding the colonial legislative power, it shall be the duty of the insular chambers:

(1) To administer to the Governor-General the oath that he will uphold the constitution and the laws which guarantee the autonomy of the colony.

(2) To make effective the responsibility of the governmental secretaries who, when accused by the chamber of representatives, shall be tried by the council of administration.

(3) To address the central Government through the governor-general in order to propose to it the abrogation or modification of the laws of the Kingdom which are in force, to request it to present drafts of laws concerning determinate matters, or to request it to adopt resolutions of an executive character on subjects which interest the colony.

ART. 30. In all cases in which, in the opinion of the governor-general, the national interests may be affected by the colonial statutes, the presentation of drafts of ministerial initiative shall be preceded by their communication to the central Government.

If the project shall be the outgrowth of parliamentary initiative, the colonial Government shall ask for the postponement of the discussion until the central Government shall have expressed its opinion.

In both cases the correspondence that has passed between the two governments shall be communicated to the chambers and shall be published in the Gazette.

ART. 31. Conflicts of jurisdiction between the different municipal assemblies, provincial and insular, or with the executive power, which owing to their nature shall not be referred to the central Government, shall be submitted to the courts of justice, in accordance with the provisions of this decree.

TITLE VI.—*Of the powers of insular parliament.*

ART. 32. The insular chambers shall have power to legislate concerning all matters that have not been specially and determinately reserved to the Cortez of the Kingdom or the central Government, according to the present decree or to the provisions that may hereafter be adopted as provided in article 2 additional.

Consequently, the enumeration presuming no limitation of their powers, it shall be their duty to decide concerning all matters that belong to the ministries of grace and justice, government, finance and fomento, in its three divisions, public works, education, and agriculture.

It shall likewise be their duty to obtain special information with regard to all matters of a purely local nature which principally affect the colonial territory; and in this sense they may decide concerning administrative organization and division, whether territorial, provincial, municipal, or judicial; concerning public health, both on sea and land; concerning public credit, banks, and the monetary system.

These powers are to be understood as not interfering with those belonging, in connection with the same matters, according to law, to the colonial executive power.

ART. 33. It shall likewise be the duty of the insular parliament to prepare the regulations for the execution of those laws enacted by the Cortes of the Kingdom that shall be expressly confided to it. In this sense it specially belongs to it (and it may do so at its very first meeting) to decide concerning electoral procedure, the preparation of the census, the qualifications of electors, and the manner in which elections shall be held; but its decisions shall in nowise affect the rights of citizens as they are recognized by the electoral law.

ART. 34. Although the laws relating to the administration of justice and the organization of the courts are of a general character, and therefore obligatory upon the colony, the Colonial Parliament may, subject to them, adopt such rules or propose to the Central Government such measures as may facilitate the entrance, retention, and promotion in the local courts of the natives of the Island, or of those who practice the legal profession there. The Governor-General in council shall exercise the powers which, as regards the appointment of legal officers, subordinates, and assistants, and as regards other matters connected with the administration of justice, are now exercised by the ministry of the colonies so far as the Island of Cuba is concerned.

ART. 35. It shall be an exclusive power of the Insular Parliament to prepare the local budget both of expenditures and receipts, and to prepare that of the receipts necessary to meet the portion of expense of the national budget which is payable by the Island.

To this effect, the Governor-General shall lay before the Chambers, before the month of January of each year, the budget for the following fiscal year, divided into two parts, the first of which shall contain a statement of the receipts necessary to meet the expenses of sovereignty; the second, the expenditures and receipts which properly belong to the colonial administration.

Neither of the chambers shall deliberate concerning the colonial budget without having definitely passed upon the portion relating to the expenses of sovereignty.

ART. 36. It shall be the duty of the Cortes of the Kingdom to decide what are to be considered, from their nature, as obligatory expenses inherent in sovereignty, and also to fix every three years the amount thereof and the receipts necessary to meet them, the Cortes having always the right to change this provision.

ART. 37. The negotiation of treaties of commerce affecting the Island of Cuba, whether they are due to the initiative of the insular government or to that of the central Government, shall always be conducted by the latter, assisted in both cases by special delegates, duly authorized by the colonial government, the conformity of which treaties to what has been agreed upon shall be shown when they are laid before the Cortes of the Kingdom.

These treaties, if they shall be approved by the Cortes, shall be published as laws of the Kingdom, and as such they shall remain in force in the territory of the Island.

ART. 38. Treaties of commerce in the negotiation of which the Insular Government shall not have taken part shall be communicated to it when they shall become laws of the Kingdom, in order that it may, within three months, declare whether it desires to adhere to their stipulations or not. In case of its desiring to adhere to them the Governor-General shall publish a statement to that effect in the Gazette as a colonial statute.

ART. 39. It shall further be the duty of the Insular Parliament to prepare the tariff and to designate the duties to be paid on goods, both when imported into the territory of the Island and when exported therefrom.

ART. 40. By way of transition from the present régime to that for which provision is hereby made, and without prejudice to what may be agreed upon at the proper time by the two Governments, commercial relations between the Peninsula and the Island of Cuba shall be governed by the following provisions:

(1) No duty, whether of a fiscal character or not, and whether established for imports or exports, shall be differential to the detriment of insular or peninsular productions.

(2) A list of articles of direct national origin shall be prepared by both Governments, for which articles there shall be established by common consent a differential duty on those similar to them of foreign origin.

In another similar list, prepared in the same manner, those productions of insular origin shall be determined which are to receive privileged treatment when imported into the Peninsula. The rate of the differential duties shall likewise be determined.

This differential duty shall in no case exceed, for both origins, 35 per cent.

If, in the preparation of both lists and in the fixing of the protective duties, there shall be an agreement between the two governments, the lists shall be considered definitive and shall be adopted at once. If there shall be any disagreement, the point in dispute shall be submitted for decision to a commission of deputies of the Kingdom, consisting equally of natives of Cuba and of the Peninsula. This commission shall choose its president. If no agreement shall be reached concerning his appointment, the oldest officer shall preside. The president shall have a vote by virtue of his office.

(3) The tables of valuations for the articles enumerated in the two lists mentioned in the foregoing number shall be adopted by common consent, and shall be revised every two years, a hearing being granted to both parties. The modifications which it shall be proper to make, in view thereof, in the tariff, shall be at once carried out by the respective governments.

TITLE VII.

ART. 41. The supreme government of the colony shall be vested in a governor-general, who shall be appointed by the King, on motion of the council of ministers. In this capacity he shall exercise, as a vice-royal patron, the powers inherent in the patronate of the Indies; he shall have the chief command of all the armed forces, both naval and military, in the island; he shall be the representative of the ministries of state, war, navy, and the colonies; all the authorities of the island shall be subordinate to him, and he shall be responsible for the preservation of order and of the safety of the colony.

The Governor-General, before assuming the duties of his office, shall make oath before the King that he will perform them faithfully and loyally.

ART. 42. The Governor-General, as the representative of the nation, shall perform by himself, and assisted by his secretaries, all the duties mentioned in the foregoing articles, and that may be incumbent upon him as the direct representative of the King in matters of a national character. It shall be the duty of the Governor-General, as the representative of the mother country:

(1) To designate freely the employees of his secretariat.

(2) To publish, execute, and cause to be executed on the island the laws, decrees, treaties, international conventions, and other instruments emanating from the legislative branch of the Government, and likewise the decrees, royal orders, and other instruments emanating from the executive branch that shall be communicated to him by the ministries, whose representative he is.

When, in his judgment, and that of the secretaries of his administration, the decisions of Her Majesty's Government might cause injury to the general interests of the nation, or to the special interests of the island, he shall suspend their publication and execution, making a report thereof and of the causes upon which his decision is based to the proper ministry.

(3) To exercise the pardoning power in the name of the King within the limits which shall have been specially marked out for him in his instructions, and to suspend the execution of capital punishment in cases in which the gravity of the circumstances may demand it, or the urgency of the case may not allow time to solicit and obtain pardon from Her Majesty, the opinion of the secretaries being heard in all cases.

(4) To suspend the guaranties named in articles 4, 5, 6, and 9, and paragraphs 1, 2, and 3 of article 13, of the constitution of the State, to enforce the laws relative to public order, and to take all such measures as he may deem necessary for the preservation of peace within, and of security outside of the territory that is intrusted to him, the council of secretaries being previously heard.

(5) To take care that justice be speedily and properly administered in the colony, in which it shall always be administered in the name of the King.

(6) To communicate directly concerning matters of external policy with the representatives, diplomatic agents, and consuls of Spain in America.

Correspondence of this kind shall be communicated in its entirety and simultaneously to the minister of state.

ART. 43. It shall be the duty of the Governor-General, as the superior authority of the island and the head of its administration:

(1) To take care that the rights, powers, and privileges recognized or hereafter to be recognized as belonging to the colonial administration, be duly respected and upheld.

(2) To sanction and publish the enactments of the insular parliament, which shall be laid before him by the president and secretaries of the respective chambers.

When the Governor-General shall consider that an enactment of the insular parliament goes beyond the powers of that body, violates the rights of citizens which are recognized in Title I of the constitution, or the guarantees fixed by law for the exercise of those rights, or jeopardizes the interests of the colony or of the State, he shall send the enactment to the council of ministers, of the Kingdom which, in a period not exceeding six months, shall approve it or return it to the Governor-General, with a statement of the reasons that it may have for objecting to its sanction and promulgation. The insular parliament, in view of these reasons, may again deliberate concerning the matter and modify the enactment, if it thinks proper, without the necessity of a special proposition.

If two months shall pass without the central Government's having expressed its opinion concerning an enactment of the Chambers that shall have been transmitted to it by the Governor-General, that officer shall sanction and promulgate it.

(3) To appoint, suspend, and remove the employees of the colonial administration, on motion of the respective secretaries of the Government, and in accordance with the laws.

(4) To appoint and remove freely the secretaries of the Government.

ART. 44. No order of the Governor-General, issued in his capacity as representative and head of the colony, shall be carried out unless it is countersigned by a secretary of the government, who, by this act alone, becomes responsible therefor.

ART. 45. The secretaries of the government shall be five:
Grace, justice, and of the interior.
Finance.
Public instruction.
Public works and means of communication.
Agriculture, industry, and commerce.

The secretary, who shall be appointed by the Governor-General, shall be president. The Governor-General may likewise appoint a president without a determinate department.

The insular parliament shall have power to increase or diminish the number of the secretaries of the Government, and also to determine what matters belong to the department of each.

ART. 46. The secretaries of the Government may be members of the chamber of representatives or of the council of administration, and take part in the discussions of both bodies; but they shall only have a vote in that to which they belong.

ART. 47. The secretaries of the Government shall be responsible for their acts to the insular chambers.

ART. 48. The Governor-General shall not modify or revoke his own orders when they shall have been sanctioned by the Government, whether they are declaratory of rights, or have served as a basis for a judicial decision, or shall have reference to his own competency.

ART. 49. The Governor-General shall not delegate the powers of his office on absenting himself from the island without the express permission of the Government.

In cases of absence from the capital, which shall prevent him from transacting business, or of the impossibility of his doing so, he may designate a person or persons to act in his stead, if the Government shall not previously have done so, or if, in his instructions, there is no provision made for the appointment of a substitute.

ART. 50. The supreme court shall take cognizance, without appeal, of all charges defined in the penal code that shall be made against the governor-general.

The council of ministers shall take cognizance of any malfeasance in office committed by him.

ART. 51. The Governor-General, notwithstanding the provisions contained in the various articles of this decree, may act by himself and on his own responsibility, without granting a hearing to the secretaries of the Government in the following cases:

(1) When the question is of the transmission to the Government of the enactments of the insular chambers, especially when he considers that the rights guaranteed in Title I of the constitution of the monarchy or the guarantees provided by law for their exercise are violated by those enactments.

(2) When the law relative to public order is to be executed, especially if there is no time or any way to consult the central government.

(3) When the question is of the execution and fulfillment of laws of the Kingdom sanctioned by His Majesty, and operative in all the Spanish territory or that of its Government.

A law shall provide for the procedure and means of action that may be used in such cases by the Governor-General.

TITLE VIII.—*Of the municipal and provincial régime.*

ART. 52. Municipal organization shall be obligatory in every center of population containing more than 1,000 inhabitants. Localities containing a smaller population may organize services of a common character by special agreements.

Any municipal board that is legally constituted shall have power to legislate concerning public instruction, communication by land, river, or sea, concerning local health, the municipal budgets, and to appoint and remove its employees at will.

ART. 53. At the head of each province there shall be a deputation, elected in the manner provided by the colonial statutes and composed of a number of members in proportion to its population.

ART. 54. The provincial deputations shall be autonomous in everything relating to the creation and dotation of establishments of public instruction and charitable institutions, provincial means of communication by land, river, or sea, the preparation of their budgets, and the appointment and removal of their employees.

ART. 55. Both the municipal boards and provinces may freely provide for the receipts necessary to meet the expenditures of their budgets without any limitation other than that of making them harmonize with the general system of taxation of the island.

The means derived from the provincial budget shall be independent of those derived from the municipal budget.

ART. 56. The councilmen elected by the municipal districts shall be alcaldes and acting alcaldes.

ART. 57. The alcaldes shall perform the active duties of the municipal administration without any limitation whatever, as executors of the enactments of the municipal governments and as their representatives.

ART. 58. Both the councilmen and the provincial deputies shall be civilly responsible for any injuries that may be caused by their acts.

They may be held thus responsible before the ordinary courts.

ART. 59. The provisional deputations shall freely choose their presidents.

ART. 60. Elections for councilmen and provincial deputies shall be held in such a manner that the minorities may be legitimately represented therein.

ART. 61. The provincial and municipal law now in force in Cuba shall continue in force so far as it is not at variance with the provisions of this decree, until the colonial parliament shall decide concerning these matters.

ART. 62. No colonial statute shall deprive the municipal boards or the deputations of the powers recognized in the foregoing articles as belonging to them.

TITLE IX.—*Of guarantees for the enforcement of the colonial constitution.*

ART. 63. Any citizen may apply to the courts when he thinks that his rights have been violated or his interests injured by the enactments of a municipal board or of a provincial deputation.

The Government attorney, if he shall be requested to do so by the agents of the colonial executive power, shall likewise prosecute before the courts any infractions of law or abuses of power that may have been committed by the municipal governments and the deputations.

ART. 64. In the cases referred to in the foregoing article the following courts shall be competent:

For complaints against the municipal boards, the superior court of the territory.

For complaints against the provincial deputations, the superior court of Havana.

These courts, when they have to decide cases of abuses of power by the aforesaid bodies, shall decide in full court. Appeal may be taken from the decisions of the territorial courts to the superior court of Havana, and from the decisions of this latter court to the supreme court of the Kingdom.

ART. 65. The privileges granted in article 62 to any citizen may be exercised collectively by means of a public action, an attorney or representative being appointed for that purpose.

ART. 66. Without prejudice to the powers granted to him in Title V, the Governor-General, when he shall think proper, may have recourse, in his capacity as head of the colonial executive power, to the superior court of Havana, to the end that that court may decide conflicts of jurisdiction between the colonial executive power and the legislative chambers.

ART. 67. If any question of jurisdiction shall arise between the insular parliament and the Governor-General in his capacity as representative of the Central Government, which, on petition of the former, shall not be submitted to the council of ministers of the Kingdom, each of the two parties may submit it for decision to the supreme court of the Kingdom, which shall decide in full court and without appeal.

ART. 68. Decisions having reference to the cases provided for in the foregoing articles shall be published in the collection of colonial statutes, and shall form part of the laws of the island.

ART. 69. Any municipal enactment having for its object the contraction of municipal loans or debts, shall have no executive force unless it shall be approved by a majority of the residents, when a demand to this effect shall have been made by one-third of the members of the municipal board.

A special statute shall determine the amount of the loan, or of the debt which according to the number of residents of the municipal district shall be necessary, in order that the case may be referred to the vote of the residents.

H. Doc. 406——6

ART. 70. All provisions of a legal character, emanating from the colonial parliament or the courts, shall be compiled under the name of colonial statutes in a legislative collection, the preparation and publication of which shall be intrusted to the Governor-General as head of the colonial executive power.

ADDITIONAL ARTICLES.

ARTICLE 1. Until colonial statutes shall have been published in due form the laws of the Kingdom shall be considered applicable to all matters that are to be acted upon by the insular government.

ART. 2. When the present constitution for the islands of Cuba and Puerto Rico shall have been approved by the Cortes of the Kingdom, it shall not be modified otherwise than by a law and at the request of the insular parliament.

ART. 3. The provisions of the present decree shall be enforced in their entirety in the Island of Puerto Rico; but in order to adapt them to the population and the nomenclature of that island they shall be published in a special decree for Puerto Rico.

ART. 4. Contracts relative to public services common both to the Antilles and the Peninsula that are in course of execution shall continue in their present form until their termination, and shall be governed in all respects by the conditions of the contract. With regard to contracts that have not yet begun to be executed, but have been already agreed upon, the Governor-General shall consult the central Government or the colonial chambers, if necessary, and the definitive form in which they shall be concluded shall be determined by common consent between the two governments.

TRANSIENT ARTICLES.

ARTICLE 1. In order to accomplish with the greatest rapidity possible, and with the least interruption of the services, the transition from the present system to that which is created by this decree, the Governor-General, when he shall think that the proper time has arrived, shall, after consulting the central Government, appoint the Government secretaries to whom reference is made in article 45, and with them shall conduct the interior government of the Island of Cuba until the insular chambers shall have been constituted.

The secretaries appointed shall cease to hold their offices when the Governor-General shall take his oath of office before the insular chambers, when they shall immediately be replaced by the Governor with persons who, in his opinion, most fully represent the majorities of the chamber of representatives and of the council of administration.

ART. 2. The manner of meeting the expenditures occasioned by the debt which now burdens the Spanish and the Cuban treasury, and that which shall have been contracted until the time of the termination of the war, shall form the subject of a law wherein shall be determined the part payable by each of the two treasuries and the special means of paying the interest thereon, and of the amortization thereof, and, if necessary, of paying the principal.

Until the Cortes of the Kingdom shall decide this point, there shall be no change in the conditions on which the aforesaid debts have been contracted, or in the payment of the interest and amortization, or in the guarantees of said debts, or in the manner in which the payments are now made.

When the apportionment shall have been made by the Cortes, it shall be for each one of the treasuries to make payment of the part assigned to it.

Engagements contracted with creditors under a pledge of the good faith of the Spanish nation, shall in all cases be scrupulously respected.

Done at the Palace, this 25th day of November, 1897.

MARÍA CHRISTINA.

PRÁXEDES MATEO SAGASTA,
President of the Council of Ministers.

COPY OF CORRESPONDENCE IN RE MAINE DISASTER.

[Telegrams.]

General Lee to Mr. Day.

HAVANA, *January 12, 1898.*

Mobs, led by Spanish officers, attacked to-day the offices of the four newspapers here advocating autonomy. Rioting at this hour, 1 p. m., continues.

HAVANA, *January 12, 1898.*

Much excitement, which may develop into serious disturbances. The trouble commenced by those who oppose autonomy, and so far is directed against those who advocate it. No rioting at present, but rumors of it are abundant. Palace heavily guarded. Consulate also protected by armed men.

HAVANA, *January 13, 1898.*

After a day and night of excitement, all business suspended, and rioting, everything quiet at this hour. City heavily guarded. Soldiers protect public squares and threatened points. Mobs shouted yesterday: "Death to Blanco and death to autonomy," while "Viva Weyler" was frequently heard. Contest between Spanish factions. Attention has not yet been directed to other issues. Heard once yesterday of a few rioters shouting a proposal to march to our consulate. Presence of ships may be necessary later, but not now.

[Telegram.]

General Lee to Mr. Day.

HAVANA, *January 13, 1898.*

Three newspaper offices, not four, as previously cabled, were attacked yesterday by Spanish officers and mob. Saw mob assault two; saw soldiers sent to protect them fraternizing with mob; two attacks were attempted to-day. I am told that troops massed inside of palace to protect Governor-General shout: "Death to autonomy! Death to Blanco!" Uncertainty exists whether Blanco can control the situation. If demonstrated he can not maintain order, preserve life, and keep the peace, or if Americans and their interests are in danger, ships must be sent, and to that end should be prepared to move promptly. Excitement and uncertainty predominates everywhere.

[Telegrams.]

General Lee to Mr. Day.

HAVANA, *January 11, 1898.*

Noon. All quiet.

HAVANA, *January 15, 1898.*

Quiet prevails.

[Telegrams.]

Mr. Day to Mr. Lee.

WASHINGTON, *January 22, 1898.*

Wire number and character naval vessels other countries now in port of Havana.

Mr. Lee to Mr. Day.

HAVANA, *January 22, 1898.*

None. Two German naval vessels are expected this month.

[Telegrams.]

Mr. Day to Mr. Lee.

WASHINGTON, *January 24, 1898.*

It is the purpose of this Government to resume friendly naval visits at Cuban ports. In that view the *Maine* will call at the port of Havana in a day or two. Please arrange for a friendly interchange of calls with authorities.

Mr. Lee to Mr. Day.

HAVANA, *January 24, 1898.*

Advise visit be postponed six or seven days, to give last excitement more time to disappear. Will see authorities and let you know result. Governor-General away for two weeks. I should know day and hour visit.

Mr. Day to Mr. Lee.

WASHINGTON, *January 24, 1898.*

Maine has been ordered. Will probably arrive at Havana some time to-morrow. Can not tell hour; possibly early. Cooperate with authorities for her friendly visit. Keep us advised by frequent telegrams.

CUBAN CORRESPONDENCE.

[Telegrams.]

Mr. Lee to Mr. Day.

HAVANA, *January 25, 1898.*

At an interview authorities profess to think United States has ulterior purpose in sending ship. Say it will obstruct autonomy, produce excitement, and most probably a demonstration. Ask that it is not done until they can get instructions from Madrid, and say that if for friendly motives, as claimed, delay unimportant.

[Telegrams.]

Mr. Lee to Mr. Day.

HAVANA, *January 25, 1898.*

Ship quietly arrived 11 a. m. to-day. No demonstration so far.

Mr. Lee to Mr. Day.

HAVANA, *January 25, 1898.*

Commanders of Spanish naval ships and of German training ship have called upon commander of *Maine* and their visits will be returned afternoon. Salutes exchanged. All quiet.

Mr. Lee to Mr. Day.

HAVANA, *January 25, 1898.*

Have just received visit of commander of *Maine* and will return it to-morrow. He had already returned official visits of Spanish and other naval officers. No disorders of any sort.

Mr. Lee to Mr. Day.

HAVANA, *January 25, 1898.*

Another German naval vessel arrived this morning. Peace and quiet reign.

[Telegrams.]

General Lee to Mr. Day.

HAVANA, *January 26, 1898.*

Have just had pleasant visit on *Maine.*

General Lee to Mr. Day.

HAVANA, *January 27, 1898.*

Just visited General Parrado, Acting Governor-General, with Sigsbee and two of his officers. We were most cordially received, and Parrado returns visit by going aboard *Maine* to-morrow.

General Lee to Mr. Day.

HAVANA, *January 28, 1898.*

Acting Governor-General Parrado and staff went with me this morning to return visit of Sigsbee. Inspected the *Maine*, were entertained and given the appropriate salute. Expressed pleasure at their reception and admiration for the splendid battle ship.

[Telegram.]

Mr. Day to General Lee.

WASHINGTON, *February 4, 1898.*

Secretary of the Navy thinks not prudent for a vessel to remain long in Havana; sanitary reasons. Should some vessel be kept there all the time? If another sent, what have you to suggest as to kind of ship? Telegraph your views.

[Telegram.]

General Lee to Mr. Day.

HAVANA, *February 4, 1898.*

Do not think slightest sanitary danger to officers or crew until April or even May. Ship or ships should be kept here all the time now. We should not relinquish position of peaceful control of situation or conditions would be worse than if vessel had never been sent. Americans would depart with their families in haste if no vessel in harbor on account of distrust of preservation of order by authorities. If another riot occurs, will be against Governor-General and autonomy, but might include anti-American demonstration also. First-class battle ship should replace present one if relieved, as object lesson and to counteract Spanish opinion of our Navy, and should have torpedo boat with it to preserve communication with Admiral.

[Telegrams.]

Mr. Lee to Mr. Day.

HAVANA, *February 5, 1898.*

Montgomery arrived Matanzas 10.30 a. m. yesterday.

General Lee to Mr. Day.

HAVANA, *February 7, 1898.*

Wrote secretary-general, asking who represented Government absence Blanco. Replied General Parrado. Captain Sigsbee and two officers accompanied me and promptly made call. Next day went with Parrado and staff on *Maine* return call. The proper salute fired for him, and they were entertained. Understood only necessary to call head of Government, just as in Washington on President and not on Cabinet or mayor of city. What omissions are charged? No one said anything to me on subject. There was certainly no intention to omit any customary courtesy.

[Telegram.]

General Lee to Mr. Day.

HAVANA, *February 11, 1898.*

Sigsbee attended General Blanco's reception with me last night. This morning paid him and others of Government officials visit.

[Telegram.]

General Lee to Mr. Day.

HAVANA, *February 16, 1898.—12.30 p. m.*

Maine blown up and destroyed to-night at 9.40 p. m. Explosion occurred well forward under quarters of crew; consequence many were lost. It is believed all officers saved, but Jenkins and Merritt not yet accounted for. Cause of explosion yet to be investigated. Captain-General and Spanish army and navy officers have rendered every assistance. Sigsbee and most of his officers on Ward steamer *City of Washington*. Others on Spanish man-of-war and in city. Am with Sigsbee now, who has telegraphed Navy Department.

[Telegram.]

General Lee to Mr. Day.

HAVANA, *February 17, 1898.*

All quiet. Great sorrow expressed by authorities. Sigsbee has telegraphed details to Navy Department. Not prepared yet to report cause of explosion.

Mr. Lee to Mr. Day.

HAVANA, *February 17.*

Profound sorrow expressed by Government and municipal authorities, consuls of foreign nations, organized bodies of all sorts, and citizens generally. Flags are at half-mast on Governor-General's palace, on shipping in harbor, and in city. Business suspended. Theaters closed. Dead will number about 260. Officers' quarters being in rear and seamen's forward, where explosion took place, accounts for greater proportionate loss sailors. Funeral to-morrow, 3 p. m. Officers Merritt and Jenkins still missing. Suppose United States naval court inquiry will be held to ascertain cause explosion. Hope our people will repress excitement and calmly await decision.

LEE.

Mr. Lee to Mr. Day.

HAVANA, *February 17.*

Merritt in junior officers' mess room. Jenkins in wardroom mess room at time explosion; latter left before an officer who was saved; must have gone wrong way. Lights out immediately; water rushing in. Merritt got to hatch with Naval Cadet Boyd. Ladder gone. Boyd climbed through and tried to pull Merritt up, but latter let go his hand, fell back, and was drowned. Bodies of these officers not found yet; probably in wreck. Sailors' funeral to-day at 3; will be immense procession.

LEE.

Mr. Lee to Mr. Day.

HAVANA, *February 18.*

Great popular demonstration at funeral yesterday; military, naval, firemen, and civil organizations generally represented. The bishop, General Parrado, second in command to Governor-General; autonomistic cabinet, civil governor, mayor, and other principal persons walked in procession part of route in accordance with custom to testify sympathy. Forty bodies buried. Many coming to surface water since, but now difficult to recognize, will be buried with religious services as collected.

LEE.

Mr. Lee to Mr. Day.

HAVANA, *February 18.*

Sigsbee begins to-morrow with divers sent to him from United States to recover all bodies still left in wreck *Maine*, as well as personal effects officers and men, and whatever else can be obtained that way. After that is completed the Spanish Government would like to unite with ours in having bottom of ship and harbor in vicinity jointly examined.

LEE.

[Telegrams.]

General Lee to Mr. Day.

HAVANA, *February 18, 1898.*

Seventy-three bodies *Maine* seamen in coffins awaiting burial in addition to forty buried yesterday.

General Lee to Mr. Day.

HAVANA, *February 21, 1898.*

Great need divers get effects and bodies from wreck; two now employed; twelve or fifteen could be used. One hundred and forty-three bodies buried. Very few found to-day. Over one hundred supposed to be confined in ship. Sailors now in two Spanish hospitals number eleven. Visited them yesterday; all will recover, except two; are comfortable and well cared for.

Mr. Lee to Mr. Day.

No. 777.] UNITED STATES CONSULATE-GENERAL,
Havana, February 18, 1898.

SIR: I have the honor to transmit herewith a translation of a communication from the Governor and Captain General, expressing sorrow for the loss of the *Maine*.

I am, sir, etc., FITZHUGH LEE,
Consul-General.

[Inclosure in No. 777.]

GENERAL GOVERNMENT OF THE ISLAND OF CUBA,
Havana, February 16, 1898.

MR. CONSUL: It becomes my painful duty to express to you my profound sorrow for the misfortune which occurred yesterday on board the American ship *Maine*. I associate myself with all my heart to the grief of the nation and of the families who have lost some of their members; and upon so doing I do not only express my personal sentiments, but I speak in the name of all the inhabitants of Havana—witnesses of the catastrophe which has afflicted so many homes.

God guard you many years.

RAMON BLANCO.

The CONSUL-GENERAL OF THE UNITED STATES.

[Telegram.]

Mr. Day to General Lee.

WASHINGTON, *February 19.*

The Government of the United States has already begun an investigation as to the causes of the disaster to the *Maine* through officers of the Navy especially appointed for that purpose, which will proceed independently. This Government will afford every facility it can to the Spanish authorities in whatever investigation they may see fit to make upon their part.

DAY.

[Telegram.]

General Lee to Mr. Day.

HAVANA, *February 22, 1898.*

Copper cylinders' ammunition found intact in 10-inch forward magazine, starboard side, this morning. Seems to show that magazine now exploded. Evidence beginning to prove explosion on port side by torpedo.

[Telegrams.]

General Lee to Mr. Day.

HAVANA, *February 25, 1898.*

Keyes was buried on 17th. Spanish law forbids exhumation bodies before expiration five years.

General Lee to Mr. Day.

HAVANA, *February 26, 1898.*

Most of the bodies buried. Some over week ago. Many unrecognizable. Against Spanish law to exhume until expiration of five years. Neither steamers nor authorities permit shipment bodies unless at once embalmed and in metallic cases. Cost between $600 and $800 each.

[Telegram.]

General Lee to Mr. Day.

HAVANA, *February 28, 1898.*

Arrangements made both Governments conduct independently investigation *Maine* disaster.

Mr. Lee to Mr. Day.

No. 782.] UNITED STATES CONSULATE-GENERAL,
Havana, February 28, 1898.

SIR: With reference to my telegram of this morning, which I now confirm, reading: "Arrangements made, both Governments conduct independently investigation *Maine* disaster," I now have the honor to transmit copies of the correspondence with this Government on the subject.

I am, sir, etc.,

FITZHUGH LEE,
Consul-General.

[Inclosure 1 in No. 782.]

GENERAL GOVERNMENT OF THE ISLAND OF CUBA,
OFFICE OF THE SECRETARY,
Havana, February 28, 1898.

In order to terminate the expediente (proceedings) of investigation initiated by the Spanish Government regarding the causes which produced the catastrophe of the *Maine*, it is only lacking to proceed to an examination of the exterior and interior part of the vessel where the explosion occurred, for which it is deemed indispensable for the better accomplishment of this object that our divers, upon performing the examination, be accompanied by those of the American Government; and inasmuch as no conclusive answer has been received from you to proceed to same, I beg you will please direct or request whoever it may concern to the effect that said divers join the Spanish divers for the purpose of making the report of the examination. I also beg to ask you to name a period of time as soon as possible.

God guard you many years.

Havana, February 25, 1898. RAMON BLANCO.

To the CONSUL-GENERAL OF THE UNITED STATES.

[Inclosure No. 2, with dispatch No. 782, Havana, February 28, 1898.]

UNITED STATES CONSULATE-GENERAL,
Havana, February 26, 1898.

To His Excellency the Governor-General of the Island of Cuba.

EXCELLENCY: I have the honor to acknowledge the receipt of your communication of the 25th instant. In reply I beg to inclose a copy of my telegram to the honorable Assistant Secretary of State at Washington in reference to the subject, and also the Department's reply.

It would be observed that the United States Government thinks that the examinations by the two Governments should proceed independently, but that every facility should be given to make whatever investigation your Government may see fit. I will confer with Captain Sigsbee on the subject and suggest that he visit the admiral of the naval station, and I have no doubt that these two officers can agree upon a plan which would be satisfactory for all concerned.

I am quite sure that neither Government has any other object except to ascertain all the facts connected with the explosion of the *Maine,* and that the great desire of both Governments is to proceed harmoniously with the work.

I am, etc.,
FITZHUGH LEE,
Consul-General.

I.P. D '09

LIBRARY OF CONGRESS

0 013 902 184 8

www.ingramcontent.com/pod-product-compliance
Lightning Source LLC
Chambersburg PA
CBHW031355160426
43196CB00007B/824